GET BRITAIN WORKING

Social Action

Karen Melonie Gould

authorHOUSE®

AuthorHouse™ UK Ltd.
500 Avebury Boulevard
Central Milton Keynes, MK9 2BE
www.authorhouse.co.uk
Phone: 08001974150

First published by AuthorHouse 4/30/2010

ISBN: 978-1-4490-8456-1 (sc)

This book is printed on acid-free paper.

Contents

Chapter 7

Chapter 8

Chapter 9

Chapter 10

Acknowledgements

Thanks to all those Professionals who firstly worked with me on the **Job Club** which was the basis of the book from 2009 until 2010.

Elizabeth Macdonald   – Warrington Job Club Coordinator
David Mowat   – Facilitator of Warrington Job Club
Steve Miller, Grab that Job   – Guru of Warrington Job Club
Marissa Hankinson, Third Marketing and Guest Speaker on E-Marketing
Paul Guy, Job Club Member   – Mentor and Guest Speaker – Psychometric Testing
David Cheetah, Business Link   – SME Business Support
Chris Cardell   – Marketing Guru
Wendy Stockton   – Image Professional Consultant
Robert Raby   – IT Consultant

ILM – Units based on Level 3 Leadership & Management

BELBIN – Guide to How to Succeed at Work

The **Job Club Members** – you know who you are who gave me the inspiration to write this book.

The **Job Club Mentors** – who supported the above Programme and in particular Phil Marshall from Shoot the Moon, Mustafa, Murdo, Sheila, David, Sham and many more.

And to my **friends and colleagues** who have supported me – and you know who you are!

My husband Fethi and my good friend Wendy and my God who encouraged me.

"This book will **Open Doors**, you will **Move On**, progress professionally and personally and hey – you **will** move on into employment as 80% of my job club programme members did !!! "

Peace – love and happiness – Karen xxx

Foreword

'GET BRITAIN WORKING'

As the Conservative Party moved forward with their above campaign our local Conservative Party Candidate for Warrington South, David Mowat, felt that it was their duty to tackle this problem locally with the increasing number of unemployment on the rise, particularly in the Executive/ Graduate and even the 50 + groups where there was little support. I knew David through our Charity work supporting young people and he asked me to write a programme to reflect supporting these Groups

I had delivered **Executive/Job clubs** in the last recession in London and **Graduate Programmes** working in partnership with DWP, JCP, Bethnal Green City Challenge, and local councils all working in partnership with the top London FTSE corporate companies from Price Waterhouse to Slaughter and May to Kleinwort Benson supported by Paul Boteng MP, as then.

I then set about using a 'trend analysis' a programme which reflected our NEW economic climate. This **Bespoke** Programme is the basis for this book – **'GET BRITAIN WORKING'.** I have to say that I changed the programme weekly as it was 'user led' and it had to reflect what the clients wanted and needed in terms of skills to successfully compete in today's job market. Since first writing this book I have modified it to reflect changes within the job market.

With over 3 million unemployed it will become more and more difficult – though there is a 'cloud with a silver lining!'

Graduates

Yes, we are in a recession and graduates face a 5.4% cut in graduate vacancies for 2009. Though, you have to get in touch – up your game – equip yourself with those latest 'tools' – your secret weapons – which can be found in this book and grab those opportunities whether it be in the Public Sector, E-Marketing etc see TOP 10 JOBS. Salaries will remain the same, around £25K – though you will still earn more than those without a degree and in any other unemployment periods to follow, you will still be ahead of your colleagues. (See for *Management and Graduate Ability Test www.shl.com*)

Career Advancement

Even though promotions will be less as companies may have to cut back on spending, for those out there who are ambitious this is your time to shine and push yourself forward. This is a time re-evaluate yourself; develop your personal effectiveness (see Personal *Effectiveness – Mentoring*). This is the time for you to check your skill set, qualifications, image, and other areas from your appraisal at work to see what your employer wants and to give it to them.

Professionals

I have seen an increasing number of **executives** on my programme from middle to senior management. This gives you the opportunity to look at your transferable skills, have a change of career and 'follow that dream' of becoming your own boss. Be a consultant to setting up your own business – (see *Setting up Your Own Business*). Having been a Consultant myself, there will be times – possibly 3 months in one year where you will not work – feast or famine – so save for a rainy day!

Been Made Redundant?

Do not take this personal – it is not you that has been made redundant but the job became redundant. You are not alone and it has happened to us all and there is not one family in the UK that is not affected by someone being made redundant at some time – my husband was made redundant – so I have been implementing this strategy with him and it worked – he got a job – albeit not the one he wanted but it is a fresh start and it reinstated his confidence and has given him the opportunity to re-evaluate his skills and look at a new career challenge.

Women Returning To Work

You may have brought up your children and now want to return to work, your partner lost their job or maybe you are a single parent who has to return to work. This is a good time to return to work with flexible hours in Retail such companies as ASDA, Tesco, Iceland and Morrisons are all recruiting. Remember to be prepared with a professional CV to reflect your transferable skills acquired whilst off work and always try to gain experience from the voluntary sector to highlight on your CV. You will also find that some Companies like Tesco and most Public Sector Companies have a family friendly scheme which is reflected in offering flexi days for taking children to dentist etc – my brother finds this particular helpful whilst working at Tesco as a Manager even wanted time off to take his family to a family Rugby Match.

50+

Not the end of your career or the world but a whole new beginning! There are many organisations which support you: PRIDE through Prince's Trust for people 50+ wanting to start their own business and now Lavender Project. Proof of this was evident in my first job club programme where more than 50% were 50+. I do not agree that this becomes a disability nor should be looked at as one as you will feel you are starting out on a negative journey before you begin – it is just another hurdle in life to overcome. I can do it – so can You! I completely reinvented myself and have never looked back. You just have to make sure that you highlight and 'showcase' all your valuable experience and skills that you have acquired – so that you 'stand out' in a competitive market.

Top Ten Companies Recruiting 2010

- Somerfields
- Barclays
- Boots

- Everest
- Hilton
- Iceland
- Unilever
- Siemens
- Co- Op Pharmacy
- Santander

What this book will do for you as the programme did for my clients is:

1. give you confidence
2. give you the tools to acquire that job
3. motivate you to strive forward to achieve a 'dream job'

You can find out more by visiting www.connectconsultancyorganisation.com and join the **Business Club or Job Club** on line for a number of programmes or simply email: karen@ connectconsultancyorganisation.com. I am always pleased to receive your comments.

I want you to sit back and enjoy the journey that this book will take you on to a new level of self-confidence – are you ready to start to feeling good about yourself? Then read on!

Once you have read through this book you will have the tools to:

- Create that impressive CV
- Write business letters
- Make application forms work for you
- Improve your Interview techniques
- Draw up your action plan
- Identify your Strengths and Weaknesses (area for improvement)
- Recognise your Transferrable skills
- Develop a marketing strategy
- Develop an employment strategy
- Create your Personal Career Development Plan
- Improve your Leadership & Management skills
- Tap into starting your own business

The Journey begins – Good Luck!

Karen

Job Centre plus – Find Your Way Back to Work

Please see the support via your JCP (see leaflets attached).

1. If you have childcare problems whilst attending this course please see your advisor at JCP and also the Return to Work Advisor.

2. If you are having concerns re; travelling expenses to this job club please speak to us and also see you JCP advisor who may ask you to complete a travel form. Also you may get help with travel expenses to interviews outside your area of residence.

3. An additional £300 may also be available to all of you for uniforms, travelling etc to support you to get back in work, see your JCP Advisor.

4. JCP has put aside £2,500 for training for any employer who takes on a new employee; speak to your JCP Advisor.

5. Discuss with your JCP Advisor the opportunities available for you to complete a Job Trial as you will be able to do this whilst retaining your benefit(s)

6. Your JCP offer free use of phones, check if you have a reliable and cheap network i.e. Talk Talk is £9 a month in some areas.

Also - Log onto www.career4me.com your own PERSONAL on line JOB CLUB!

HOUSE OF COMMONS
LONDON SW1A 0AA

GET BRITAIN WORKING

Social Action

Get Britain Working
www.getbritainworking.com

Dear Colleague,

As you will be aware, at our conference we launched our Get Britain Working paper, detailing the action that a Conservative government will take to tackle Labour's jobs crisis, which has seen almost 2,000 people a day lose their job.

However, we are not simply waiting to win an election in order to take action. We are championing a new job search engine developed by Zubed, a UK-based software development company, as part of our on-going Get Britain Working campaign. There are currently over 230,000 jobs on the free search engine so I am very keen to spread the word around the country.

Since January Conservative candidates, MPs and councillors have been setting up Job Clubs across the country to help local people who have lost their jobs in the recession. It has become very clear to those running Job Clubs that people searching for jobs need a means of finding out about work local to them in a quick and simple way. The free to use Zubed Job Search Engine located at www.getbritainworking.com can be used to either find a job if you are looking for work or to post a job if you are an employer looking for new staff. It also has over a million volunteering opportunities for those who want to improve their skills and help their communities whilst job seeking.

Please do consider pointing your constituents towards the website if they approach you for advice on finding a job. You may also wish to bring the service to the attention of local businesses. I would be very grateful if you could encourage those running your association website to post a link to www.getbritainworking.com using the graphic attached to this email and to promote the website address to local members. I would also encourage all colleagues to post a link to the site on their personal websites. (Please note that this is a Conservative Party website so should not be linked to from a website funded by parliamentary allowances).

Thank you in advance for your help in raising awareness of this fantastic free tool.

Yours sincerely,

Rt Hon Theresa May MP
Shadow Secretary of State for Work & Pensions

Get Britain Working

Introduction to "GET BRITAIN WORKING'

Suggested tools:

A healthy body is a healthy mind and I advise that you take 8 minutes a day to embark on that new you - I am?

www.ultimatmatebootcamp.co.uk

- See your Local DWP SPORTS for special rates.
- Essential books: 'Go Grab That Job" by Steve Miller as seen on Breakfast TV
  'Succeeding at Work- a guide" by Belbin
  Professor Christopher Bones, Dean of Business School
- Monthly magazines; PSYCHOLOGIES – Watch out for my articles and request your Life Change Planner!
- Job Centre; Grab your free copy of INSPIRE magazine
- Skills Plus; www.allmerseyside.net
- Associations/Memberships; ILM Membership gives you a free EDGE magazine from the Institute of Leadership and Management.

I strongly suggest that you join the above to receive all the benefits and support that it offers.

The world is changing and sometimes we want to shout out, 'let me get off' but we don't!

You never know what is around the corner and if I could predict the future – I would have another change of career – but this one is not for me as I cannot predict the future. However **I can put you on a road full of confidence and you will project a new you** – having a new lease of life, come on you deserve it!

You must be versatile and open to change and be flexible. It is a fast pace out there and if you stand still you will not have the standard of living or lifestyle you deserve.

You are now unemployed, facing unemployment or thinking about a career change – whichever. This proven PROGRAMME as featured in this book has already produced 78% positive outcomes into to work will now take you there. It has been researched, changed with circumstances and, being user led, changed to suit the needs of you, the client. It is a practical guide which will change your life for the better!

Testimonials (from clients)

Murdo MacDonald, Appleton

"Karen, through this programme, has helped me in my social networking to establish new contacts to establish my own business."

Glenn Jones, Orford

"This Programme has given me the confidence to start a course in Management Logistics in Sept 09 and look for a career in management after years of being an unhappy heavy goods driver".

Sham Malik, Warrington

"Much needed advice in this economic climate which helped me to secure my job in Law and I will be continuing this journey by starting on the Mentoring Programme in Sep 09 re my own personal development".

Dewi Williams, Warrington

"The extended session on interviews on Saturday followed by Mustaphs's pep talk on Sunday really helped set me up for this. I wanted to say a big "Thank You" to you, the mentors and fellow job seekers for the advice and support they have given me over the last few months"

As I have said before, the job club helped maintain my confidence and kept my enthusiasm going for the job search which I think is as important as the practical advice and coaching. I am also very grateful for the practical advice I received from yourself, Murdo, Mustapha as well as the general exchange of ideas on a Saturday morning. Let me know if you need any particular format for the testimonial.

How can one put into words the expression of gratitude, so it is with only a simple but a heartfelt THANK YOU, that I send this message.

I am not one to gush etc, well unless Ive had a few too many Gin & Tonic's?

So I would just like to say, on this first Saturday morning knowing that we will not be meeting as usual, it has been a privilege to have met truly wonderful people, who not only gave up their precious time to attend, but provided support and hopefully their continued encouragement as we all face the same road to whatever dreams we aspire to do with the rest of our lives. Without their knowledge, skills and experiences of each of the Job Club programme team, they have enabled this programme to be a great success.

2   *Karen Melonie Gould*

It inspired me so much, that even though I joined the programme halfway through and after only attending one session, I volunteered to become a mentor and look forward to joining the team in their continued quest in providing future attendees a supporting network.

Well on that note, I would just like to offer my congratulation's, best wishes and good luck to you all. Keep in touch and should you need any advice on interviewing tips etc, please do not hesitate to drop me an email. Mind you not sure I'm the best not come to, as I was late for my interview yesterday??? Just hope like Dewi, they pass over that and want to see me again?

All the very best to you all.
Sheila

I have been involved with the Job Club as a mentor since its early days. Its success has exceeded my expectation: close to 80% of the candidates have found employment or started their own businesses. Such as a result would be the envy of many commercial outplacement companies!

This success would not have been possible without Karen who prepared and delivered the training. In fact Karen went beyond the call of duty by providing caring, enthusiastic and energetic coaching and mentoring. More than that, on a weekly basis, she took the time to search for opportunities which she shared with all through her her weekly e-mail alerts."

Mustafa
Mentor

would to thank you all for the help and support you have gave me over the last few weeks, and are continuing to do so

I would like to give Karen and the team a big thank you for all their hard work

As a mentor I would like to thank David Casdagli in particular, he was a fantastic mentor, and has become a valued friend I believe, to both myself and his other prodigy David Keeley.

A big thank you to Dave for the lifts into and home from the club. Dave has become a good friend who I will continue to be in contact with now the club has finished.

Ben Fitzpatrick

The Job Club, run by Mrs Karen Gould, under the auspices of the S. Warrington Conservative Association, is demonstrably effective. The "re-entry into work" rate is most praiseworthy in the present climate, thanks in no small measure to the.informative and well structured course content. As Mentor I have noticed a substantial and beneficial change in both attitude and morale amongst all the participants as the course progressed and this in turn has lead to enhanced opportunities for all concerned."

David Casdagli
Mentor

Personal Profile

I am a people's person and believe that I can 'bring out the best' in anyone and over the years have written and assisting in creating and delivering many training manuals from:

Blacon — Social Enterprise Programme
NWDA — Mentoring through the North West for Business Development
BGCC — Graduate City Programme
Connexions — Advanced Training in East London
SHDWA First and Second Steps
UCLAN Northern Lights Programme
Risley Prison Sense in the Community
YMCA Real Life Skills for 19-25yr old Disadvantaged Young People
UCLAN University Redeployment Programme
Response to Redundancy Executive Programme
Mentoring, Coaching within Leadership & Management ILM Diploma level3 for the Conservative party.

From working at **UCLAN as a Business Mentor on their Northern Lights Programme** it demonstrated that there was a lack of 'soft' skills and communication skills that very talented people seem to have acquired. It was a similar story when I delivered a **Graduate Programme in London** during the last recession, when I worked in partnership with City's **Top FTSE Companies**. I developed a training programme which reflected those skills that they wanted to see in their graduates — so very little has changed — except the introduction of E-Marketing and more social networking sites.

Whether you are a Graduate who is looking for your first job, a graduate from last year, an executive, a women returning to work or more recently those who have been made redundant or those facing redundancy — this is **the read of the year** for you.

It will make even those who are ambitious and focussed to make changes and changes begin now — it is based on facts, real life clients and experiences. So, read on — you won't be able to put it down!

I d a r e y o u!

Mentoring - An Introduction

Comes from the Greek Mythology

Being a qualified and well experienced Mentor through Institute of Leadership & Management (ILM) and a Business Mentor at UCLAN on their Northern Lights Programme, Prince's Trust – Business Start Ups for 25-30 year olds and various other programmes, I have used two techniques to assist me in facilitating a Programme:

SIROLLI Method

This enables **Enterprise** to move forward. I used this method of Mentoring for each client offering them the opportunity of having a Mentor in their chosen career or indeed some chose a Mentor that they identified could enable them to start up their own SME.

Personal Effectiveness

Using a two pronged approach this method was used to develop, individually, the client's communication skills through personal development.

The clients on the Job Club Programme were given 1 hr per week over 10 weeks of both of the above.

What is Mentoring?

It is to encourage and support our clients to develop their own individual development through a journey from being unemployed to being 'back in the game' and considered for employment and thus securing employment. We concentrate on maximising their potential and showcasing their skills, improving their performance and lead them onto becoming the person they what to be.

It gives EMPOWERMENT to people for them to progress and is an effective tool and this becomes a CONTRACT between 2 people to fulfil the client's potential and is based upon trust between the Mentor and the Mentee. I feel it does help if the Mentor has shared similar experiences which they can draw upon and I certainly use as an 'edge' in my mentoring.

The Mentor

Must gain empathy, trust and respect with the Mentee and be understanding of the Mentee's position. The Mentor should boost the confidence of the Mentee and install the feeling of 'self believe'. Demonstrate strategies to explore and encourage new ideas. Everything must be done in the strictest confidence!

The Mentee

Has the opportunity to explore new ideas, to look more closely at themselves and explore those hidden aspirations. To become more self aware and take the responsibility for your actions - self promote yourself to deliver and achieve. It is your chance to 'TAKE CONTROL'!

Mentoring is;

- Completed in the strict confidence
- Establishes a set of boundaries/rules
- Limited paperwork
- Offers flexibility
- Motivating
- Inspiring
- Challenging
- Mentee takes control and makes decisions and takes action.

A typical session should consist of:

- An introduction to the partnership between the Mentor and the Mentee to establish rapport
- Mentee then states their ground. /case
- They agree areas to be discussed
- At the end of the session the Mentor agrees an Action Plan with Mentee for next session.
- Mentor makes recommendations with Mentee agreeing and Mentor records their comments.

This FORM is then signed by both as a CONTRACT and a date is agreed to meet again,

*Note: There are various ways of Mentoring –Face to face, Group work, Telephonic, E mail, Text – indicate which in each session.

Mentor will keep up regular contact with Mentee before next meetings as agreed by whatever method both agreed. I prefer emailing and this as a way of e-learning.

Once you have got over the first session – the rest just flows. Though, I find that if you arrive at a session and the Mentee has not actioned the agreed Plan then the Mentee has not honoured their contract and you would have to consider whether you have established rapport or empathy.

I have never had this happened to me and I have avoided this by contacting the Mentee before the session by email, followed up by a call to establish boundaries and what will be expected of the Mentee. At any time, either party can decide whether or not to continue with the Partnership.

To bring this Partnership to conclusion – I allow the Mentee to draw a line under the contract and let them state that they no longer need the Mentor and that they have achieved what was agreed in their Action Plan.

GET BRITAIN WORKING

Social Action

Successful Coaching and Mentoring - Business Partners – Ken Lawson – A guide book

Strengths and Weaknesses (Areas for Development)

Psychometric Testing – Selby & Mills

This is a phenomenal in the UK in recruiting. It is an integral part of the hiring process. It is due to the high cost of recruitment and helps the employer make the right choice!

These are **Personality Questionnaires** and you can improve your **Employability** by receiving **coaching** on this and of course – plenty of practice!

Companies are using these to:
* Select their right type of person i.e. Team player
* Personality traits i.e. Team player

They use **Occupational Psychologists** to compile this information. Your answers are interpreted by Test Administrators in HR and they conclude **facts** about you based on your answers.

We are going to work as a Team to identify your Strengths & Weaknesses (Areas for development) and will compare this from your online test and from your Appraisal at the end of this Programme to see if you have gained more strengths and now how fewer weaknesses!

Please log on to; www.selbymills.co.uk/careers/strengths/weaknesses and for the next 20 minutes this will focus on:

Customer service skills
People management skills
Business Quality – Management skills
Professional skills

You can also purchase a "Management Potential - 64 Questions" at a cost of £14.95 and which will take you around 10 minutes to complete.

Though, if you register with a reputable Agency in your field of work they will complete these for you.

So, after this Introduction you will not be anxious about these again! Will you?

Conclusion

At the end of this Programme you will be able to rapidly answer the questions in the safe knowledge that your chances of employment remain intact!

You should not be job searching7 days a week as 2 days a week should be used to showcase your skills to make a difference – learning new skills and meeting new people and making new contacts it is better than watching day time TV.

Get out there – they need your skills and you need their support, Good Luck!

Volunteering – What's in it for you?

People take part in Volunteering for various reasons and on this Programme you should engage up to 16 hrs of Volunteering work per week in line with JCP guidelines re your benefits to:

- Gain valuable work experience in a certain field or new field
- Meet new people – social networking
- Develop existing skills or learn new ones
- Enjoy a sense of personal achievement
- Have something positive to put onto your CV
- Make use of any spare time
- Have a strong affinity to a certain cause and want to make a difference
- Work as part of a team and have lots of fun and enjoyment

Volunteering will give you a great deal of satisfaction in the knowledge that you are really making that difference!

There are various opportunities and you can choose an area of interest;

See your local www.cvs.org.uk or www.info@vc.org.uk

Whether it is IT skills and your interest is to work in Mental Health, then contact Mental Health Forums for a list of organisations in your area. Some of your local authorities will have a database of the voluntary organisations listed with vacancies or contact your local CVS centre.

CV Preparation

This is an introduction to creating that CV which will do you proud!

CV comes from the Latin meaning Course for Life and highlights your skills/experience

Using my format, which I have used with Morgan Hunt Recruiters and which has done me proud for the last 5 years and secured 4 out of 5 interview opportunities for me, please pay attention to the:

- Style and presentation
- Use 8 sections; put heading in bold and aim to put information on to 2 pages.
- Spelling and grammar. It is imperative to get someone to proof read **before** you send it off and make use of your spell check – any CV sent with mistakes in either is usually binned!

Your CV is your passport to success and to securing that interview - Then you are on your way!

Remember that competition is fierce and in the economic climate jobs are fewer and fewer. You need to make sure that your CV is not;

- Overlooked
- Passed by
- Fails to impress
- Binned

Section 1– Name and address

This needs to be in full with correct postal code. It has to include your telephone numbers both home and mobile and your email address – then they should have no trouble in getting hold of you quickly to discuss an interview date!

Section 2 – Personal Profile

Please highlight:

- Skills and qualities
- Career aims

In 6/10 lines be specific to the job you are applying for – you can change this section to highlight the job description each time.

Example;

If it is to work with people say you are a good team player and an effective communicator and keep it brief.

Karen Melonie Gould

Section 3 – Key Skills

Use bullet points, be positive and clearly label your most up-to-date skills to secure the job you want.

6-10 Points would be fine!

Example

If you have experience in fundraising state what type, from donor was it SRB, ESF,ERDF, Corporate etc – anything that is specific to you area

Section 4 – Achievements

List 2to4 things you have achieved in your work/community life related to your work history and job.

Example

If you want to work for a Charity or in the Third Sector

- You organised the Warrington Homeless Christmas Ball in partnership with Warrington Wolves in 2007.

Section 5 – Employment History

Always in reverse order with your last job first – going back 10 years. NB Please do double check when completing an application form as just sometimes they want the order to be by year starting with when you left school/college/university

Example

Dates to and from   Establishment/Company Title/Job description

Section 6 – Education & Training

In reverse order with most recent first.

Example

Dates   Establishment   Subject/Qualification Grade

Include in the above any additional WORK RELATED TRAINING or COURSES whether internal or external

Example; First Aid Training, ECDL Training

Section 7 – Hobbies and Interests

These are PERSONAL but don't list too many as this could indicate you would not have time for your work. Have a good balance and highlight some family activities, community, social, sports and relaxation.

Never lie about this as you could get someone interviewing you who is an avid reader of CRIME and that is what you stated – be honest and factual!

Section 8 – References

I always put "supplied on request" because you may not want your Referees being contacted all the time – only when you have THAT JOB!

You, can today in preparation, create a separate page with:

Four references; 2 work related and 2 character giving;

- Name
- Address
- Contact numbers
- E mail address

If it is an employer then submit their full title. Try to influence and be ahead of your competition, use people high up within the company but who know your capabilities.

For a character reference use people within the community that are impressive but only if they have known you personally for more than 3 years – MPs, Councillors etc

Now You are ready to produce that master piece – Good Luck!

CV 1 Option – suitable more for technical industries.

Dewi Roland Williams
Address
Postcode
Tel number

A highly professional **Quality Manager** with specific expertise in quality assurance, product safety and evaluating and testing consumer products. Possesses extensive experience in establishing and managing effective quality systems, and UKAS accreditation as well as interpreting legislation, standards and technical documentation.

Career History

2007 – 2009   **Ultimate Products Ltd – Importers of consumer goods for retailers and Supermarkets – Senior Quality Assurance Technologist**

- Formally documented product requirements allowing the buying team a formal product benchmark, thereby substantially reducing product development time and improving customer service.
- Documented product defect classification lists for use by shipment inspectors to a common standard thus enabling them to be interpreted more easily and ensuring consistency.
- Presented in house training to colleagues on QA issues and procedures.
- Dramatically reduced both costs and time spent testing electrical products for RoHS compliance by the introduction of a portable XRF Analyser for in-house testing.
- Developed product expertise in furniture, memory foam products, toys and home wares including ceramics, cutlery and cookware.
- Evaluated new products for quality as well as compliance with legal requirements such as the General Product Safety Directive, RoHS, REACH, Packaging Waste Regulations as well as product specific requirements.

2007 – 2007   **RMS International Importers and Distributors of Consumer Goods Quality Assurance Manager – 4 month contract.**

- Successfully managed a UKAS surveillance visit resulting in renewal of laboratory UKAS accreditation.

2005 – 2006   **Bureau Veritas Consumer Product Services Hardlines Manager**

- Substantially reduced overdue jobs from 56% of work in progress to 91.5%, which also improved customer service.
- Negotiated project specifications and commercial terms with clients.
- Developed a new business activity for the company by researching and pioneering a series of tests which satisfied the BSI and the Road Traffic Act in terms of newly introduced standards for bicycle safety.
- Enhanced the company's reputation as a source of expert advice which helped to generate business in a new product area.

1990 – 2005   RMS International
Quality Assurance Manager

- Established the company laboratory and QA department for product evaluation and certification leading to:
  a. Significant reduction in turn-around time and testing costs compared to using 3rd party laboratories.
  b. Faster and more effective resolution of complaints from both customers and Trading Standards.
  c. Improvement in the company's reputation as a responsible supplier with both customers and Trading Standards Officers from various Local Authorities.
- Documented the laboratory quality manual and associated procedures leading to a successful application for UKAS accreditation.
- Maintained the laboratory quality system including document control, internal and external audits and quality checks, equipment calibration and surveillance visits by UKAS auditors.
- Developed and implemented new test methods based on product standards and updated methods and procedures in line with changes in standards and legislation.
- Monitored standards, legislation and EC Directives and advised the company on how they applied to the product range.
- Successfully developed in-house expertise to assist the buying team in product development and resolving customer queries.

1989 – 1990   Astor Chemical
Research and Development Chemist

1989 – 1989   Conoco
Shift Chemist

Professional Qualifications

Member of Royal Society of Chemistry
Member of the Institute of Quality Assurance
IQA Quality Assurance Management Qualification – University of Salford
BSC Hons Applied Chemistry – Nottingham Trent University

Training

Courtroom Skills Course – Bond Solon
Auditing in UKAS laboratories – ERA Technology
Safety Development Certificate – ROSPA

Interests

- Chief Safety Officer for firework display at annual School PTA event
- Chief Marshall at Appleton Thorn Bawming Day
- TVR Owners club member
- Maintaining physical fitness through cycling and visiting the gym

Careers Advice

Our 'GURU' mentor for this programme and who I have based this on is Steve Miller! His book, for your reading is 'Get off your arse and grab that new job"!

His top tips for us are:

1. Remember, it's the job that became redundant not you, do not take it personally
2. Sharpen up your CV – it showcases your transferable skills
3. Surround yourself with people who boost your confidence and those who can support you to greater heights.

Additional books I would recommend for developing your skills:

- The Secret by Rhonda Byrne
- The Business Stripped Bare by Richard Branson
- Wake up and change your life by Duncan Bannatyne
- How to pass the new police selection by Harry Tolley, Billy Hodge and Catherine Tolley

CV 2 Option

For those of you with only the last 3 years personal development.

Name

Address- include postcode

Contact numbers – try to include land line

E mail address

Personal Profile

6 lines only of "what I do now, what I'm looking for and what I want to do".
Do not use the 3rd person!

Professional Education

Your personal development over the last 3 years

Key Skills

Evidence based on last jobs over the last 10 years

Significant Achievements

Minimum of 3 and preferably employment based

Karen Melonie Gould

Employment

Influence, demonstrate your successes and skills, capabilities and potential
(in order of the most recent first)

Dates to and from   Organisation/Company Job title/Brief description
Name and Address

Education/Training

(in order of most recent first)

Dates to and from   Establishment/college   Course title/Grade/Pass
Name and address

Leisure Interests

6 – 10 most recent hobbies/interests

For example:

Karen Melonie Gould
Address
Tel number
k.gould@hotmail.co.uk

PERSONAL PROFILE

An accomplished Business Development Manager with extensive knowledge in Strategic Project Management, commissioning and regeneration in education & training working in partnership, securing bids/tenders for business development. I am self-motivated, innovative and a pro-active thinker. Working to strategic objectives I deliver outcomes to reflect cohesive partnerships within a community framework.

PROFESSIONAL EDUCATION/TRAINING

Sep 09	University of Chester	MBA – Business Admin
July 09	ILM Institute	Tutor/Trainer/Member
Oct 08	Coaching Academy	Life Coaching
July 08	Princes Trust	Mentoring Programme
Jan 08	North West Network	Volunteer Management

KEY SKILLS

- Strategic Project Management – Lean/ILM
- BSU/Business Development – Social Enterprise development
- Fundraising bid/tender expertise - lottery – ESF – ERDF – SRB – Corporate
- Outstanding interpersonal/communication skills – Social Networking
- Research and development – Policy/Procedures
- Management of teams re Training & Development
- Accomplished business acumen - set-up and developed own/others
- Organisational flair and co-ordination expertise – Corporate Events
- PR ability and knowledge based with E- Marketing
- Extensive training experience- created and delivered CTP/PD Programmes
- Assessing/.Monitoring/evaluating skills - DASHBOARD
- Creating and Managing budgets, monitoring, tracking – SAP, PMS
- ICT skills – Word, Excel, Databases, Spreadsheets, SAP, Delphi, Citrix

SIGNIFICANT ACHIEVEMENTS

- Book Launch – 2010 – 'GET BRITAIN WORKING' MENTORING – PERSONAL EFFECTIVENESS -
- Executive/Graduate/Business Start Up Programmes – created/delivered – 75% outcome
- Responsible for the setting-up/business development of several SME's - 2008/09 – including my own Company and receiving an 'OUTSTANDING' Ofsted Report at UCLAN.

Karen Melonie Gould

EMPLOYMENT HISTORY

April 09 – Present   Interim Projects – Executive/BSU/Development/ ILM Mentoring Programmes – Tenders/Bids – Business & Marketing/Fundraising Strategy Plans – created and deliver the 'GET BRITAIN WORKING' campaign for Conservative Party – have achieved a 75% overall outcome

Sep 09 – Nov 09   Blue Orchid – Temp Projects Manager – LSC – ESF - R2R – Graduate – BSU and Executive Programmes for North West - £10m Budget

Nov 08 – April 09   Manchester City Council; Project Manager/Commissioner - Creating a new Model of Commissioning in Children's Services/Youth - Budgets £4m/fundraising support for 26 Projects

Aug 08 – Nov 08   Warrington Borough Council – 14-19 Diplomas – Events – RAKI – organised event for 12000 pupils

Oct 07 – Nov 09   UCLAN – Northern Lights Programme – BSU/Development Training – OUTSTANDING OFSTED REPORT

Mar 07 – May 08   YMCA/Warrington – Business/Fundraising Development & Training Manager – Created and maintained Projects – Charity Events – Homeless Charity Ball – raised £25K – Bids/Tenders – City & Guilds Training

Apr 06 –Mar 07   Manchester City Council - Senior Communications Officer – Maintained and problem solved educational/training issues

Mar 05 – Mar 06   SHWDA – Fundraising and Training Manager – Created 1ST 2ND Steps Training for women – DV/A

May 04 – Feb 05   Liverpool Vision – Community Regeneration Officer – Co-ordinated City of Light, Japanese and other Events/Programmes

Sep 98 – Apr 04	Advanced Training	Director – Training & Business
	Gold Introductions	Development/ Social Networking
Mar 00 – Mar 01	LETEC/Connextions	Education/Training Consultant
Sep 99 – Apr 00	East London City Challenge	Graduate Training Consultant
Oct 98 – Sep 99	Tower Hamlets Council	Training & Development Officer
Aug 90 – Sep 98	Hackney Council	Community Training Manager

LEISURE/HOBBIES

Aerobics – swimming – dancing – fashion – music – reading – travel - socialising

Psychometric Testing

Widely used in all organisations now from ASDA to KMPG, from Marks & Spencer's to NWDA.

It is a REPORT based on your interpreting data supplied by you by answer questions from being given choices and from your answers will provide the employer with a trend in your attitude.

An example would be the format used by ASDA/TESCO which is a small A5 booklet with several questions and given choices, this is to reflect whether you would fit into a team at one of their stores. It is not a TEST – but does need honest answers reflecting team work.

Whilst at NWDA this came in the form of an on-line 45 minute multiple choice questionnaires. This together with a CV/Application form was used as a selection process for interview. Prior to the interview, a whole morning would be spent on various tests from IT, English, Maths before demonstrating your IT skills within a group situation relating to Team work – this was prior to the your Presentation and Interview.

Selby & Mills is the most common form of this testing – see info@selbymills.co.uk – most now charge for this service which on average is around £25. You need to practice these as frequently as possible and employers do unfortunately spend considerable money and time evaluating this information – so you need to get it right. Or www.magerison McCann Team Management.com

This Test will produce evidence of various heading from "STRIVING FOR SUCCESS" to "THINKING AND ACTING AHEAD!"

Additional reading;

Peter Honey – Honey and Mumford Learning Styles – www.peterhoney.com

For a learning styles Profiler with self –development feedback report –free – www.cymeon.com

Also Chris Jackson – Explores the effectiveness of the Jackson Hybrid Model of Learning in Personality.

Word of note

I used to be too analytical when attempting these and really scared – now after much practice I have noticed my learning journey with this and keep all past tests and have noticed now that I score well above average – so I am now confident in this task.

Business Letters

Used to compliment your CV
Example 1

18 Sharp Street
Warrington
WA2 7EN

Tel; 000000000

16 April 2009

Sue Young
HR Officer
Apple Mac
The Grange
Woolston
Cheshire
CH4 7DL

Dear Ms Young
Re: HR Manager vacancy

With reference to the above advertisement in the Warrington Guardian, dated 16 April 09, I have pleasure in submitting my CV for your attention.

I look forward to hearing from you with regards to an interview.

Yours sincerely

Karen Gould (Ms)

Enc: 1 (this would be a copy of your CV)

Informal Business Letter – Supporting Statement

18 Sharp Street
Warrington
Cheshire
WA2 7EN
Tel; 0000000000

9 May 2009

Sue Smith
Director
Children's Trust
13 Oxford Street
Warrington
WA1 7EN

Dear Sue
Re: Fundraising Director

With reference to the above position and our conversation today, I have pleasure in enclosing my CV for your attention.

I have been working in the Public/Third Sector for 20 years within the Community and have worked at Management level in fundraising in the following areas:

- Donor – Gift and Corporate Fundraising – engaging local companies to donate gifts through setting-up of web and general Mail Shots – using databases. Also, contacting local and national entrepreneurs to contribute. This can be done through the National Lottery website.
- ESF, SRB, ERDF, LSC, JCP, Lottery, NRF etc – I have been preparing bids for over 20 years and have had numerous successes and lately have managed to secure funding via ERDF, LSC, ESF.

I work on a Fundraising Strategy based on the organisation's Business Plan reflecting 3-7 years and would act on Funding Alerts appropriate to the organisation.

I have secured many Lottery Bids and other funding through other organisations such as Lloyds TSB, Coalfields, NWDA, Tudor Trust, Esmee Foundation and so on.

This year I worked at Manchester Council as a Consultant in Commission/Project Management and supported advising the Third Sector in identifying additional funding streams.

I also use my organisational flair to organise Corporate Events and last year organised the 14-19 Diploma Agenda in Warrington for over 13,000 children and the year before coordinated the Homeless Charity Ball in Partnership with Warrington Wolves Rugby Club.

I am looking forward to taking our discussion further and displaying my suitability for the above post at an interview.

Yours sincerely

Karen Gould (Ms)
k.gould@hotmail.co.uk
(Mobile; 07906973032)

Karen Melonie Gould

Following are 4 different letters for 4 different types of approach.

In all cases, except for the Chain letter, you should do your utmost to obtain the name, initials, title and mode of address (i.e. Mr, Mrs,Ms etc) of the appropriate person to whom you will be writing.

- G Smith HR Director and Dear Mr Smith is much more impressive that HR Director Dear Sir – and in any case it could well be a Madam.!!
- Remember also that to go with the "Reply to Advertisement" and probably the "Targeted Speculative" letters and you will need to "tune" the "standard" CV that you are attaching in order to support your letter. This will usually involve modifying your personal profile, relisting your skills and achievements and altering the batting order of the bullet points concerning your last 2 jobs.

In answer to a specific advertisement always read the advertisement carefully, several times. Underline the skills and experience they are looking for. Then look to see if there are any other features which they do not mention but which might be applicable and where you have something to offer.

- Before responding, look up the Company on the internet to see what useful information you can glean.

82 Chapel Lane
Warrington
Cheshire
CHE 3LX

Tel; 01925 00000000
E mail:

8th September 2009

M Smith
Director Human Resources
Blank Company Ltd
…………………..
…………………..

Dear Mr Smith
Vacancy for …………..

I am responding to your advertisement in the ………….. of …….

I enclose my CV from which you will notice that I match the specific criteria you are requiring, having the following relevant experience and skills…………………………….. (keep this short –they can read the detail in the CV.)

May I also mention, since it would seem that your product has an international application, that I do speak fluent French, German and Spanish and have been resident in both France and Germany.

I look forward to meeting with you.

Yours sincerely,

The So-Called Chain Letter

This is the type of letter you should write following a recommendation from a friend or colleague. ALWAYS do your utmost to leave the meeting with a name of someone else to whom you can write a similar letter.

As Above

Dear Mr Jones

I was talking recently to Charles Cornwall and he suggested that you would be someone who could be very helpful in giving me advice with respect to my future career direction.

I enclose my CV and really would be most grateful for a short amount of your time and for any advice and guidance you can give me.

I will ring you in a few days time to arrange a mutually convenient appointment.

Yours sincerely,

Karen Melonie Gould

The Targeted Speculative Letter

This is for use where you have heard/read something about a company which leads you to believe that there might be an opening for someone with your skills.

As above

Name
Title
Address
Dear

I noticed from an article in yesterday's Daily Telegraph that your company has been successful in taking its products into the .... market and have recently taken on an additional........May I congratulate you on the results of your innovative approach.

I enclose a copy of my CV because I believe that the skills and experience that I can offer may well be directly relevant to the further expansion of your business, specifically............................. (again keep this BRIEF)

I will ring you in a few days time and would hope that we can arrange a short meeting to explore options.

Yours sincerely,

The purely Speculative Letter

This is essentially "flying a kite" to a company, which whilst not overtly advertising for staff at present, might be able to make use of your transferrable skills.

As above

Name
Title
Address
Dear ....

I am writing to you, enclosing my CV, in the hope that the skills and experience that I possess will be of use to your company.

In the light of my background, skills and achievements I feel that I could be of service in the role of, for example, ... but of course there may well be other relevant opportunities within your organisation.

I will ring you in a few days time to discuss what options might be available.

Yours sincerely

Personal Profile for Karen Gould

I have had over 20 years experience in the Third Sector/Public/Community Sector embracing the Corporate Sector as major Stakeholders in the community as part of my Community Regeneration knowledge and experience.

I am a qualified and experienced Further Education Tutor/Trainer/Mentor/Coach who has developed to become a strategic Project Manager delivering to exceed targets. I compliment these skills with my extensive Fundraising success through investigative research and 15 years experience of bid/tender processes in all areas.

Recent Bids/Tenders/Training Programmes I have recently worked on are:

- Sense in the Community for Young Offenders/Offenders
- Real Life Skills for 16-25yr olds from disadvantaged groups and areas
- Learning Skills Council Redeployment Programme for UCLAN
- DWP Higher level Skills Programme – Job Search
- Social Enterprise Programmes
- Leadership & Management – Coaching and Mentoring.

I am presently a **Business Mentor** for the Prince's Trust and UCLAN University and I am a **Board Member** of a thriving Youth Charity in the North West. I also act as a **Consultant** to the Conservative Party on Youth and Employment issues within Cheshire.

With extensive knowledge of **Commissioning,** particularly in the **Third Sector** I have used my 'outstanding' networking and communication skills to drive forward Capacity Building within the sector. I have used this knowledge to work with Manchester city Council (MCC) and the PCT 08/09 working within the voluntary sector.

More recently I have become a member of ILM as a Tutor/Trainer, mentoring and coaching for the Leadership & Management Diploma at Level 5, units of which I have been incorporating and delivering in my recent Programme and which I will be used in my next book – **Mentoring – Personal Effectiveness.**

Through the Conservative Association in partnership with local businesses I created and delivered a Job Search Programme with Mentoring and SME Business support in partnership with Business Link and have achieved a 78% success rate – 10/13 into employment. I conducted a Radio Show phone in re Job/Training/Educational opportunities during the Summer of 09 and am in talks with the BBC about a documentary on Job Search in the North West

I have also been working as a Consultant with SME's in R2R – Executive – Graduate and Business Start ups and am working on various bids and tenders re business development for local SME organisations.

With this book due to be launched in Dec 2009, **"Get Britain Working'** has within it the elements of **Mentoring** as a support mechanism to secure **Employment** through jobs or SME.

My second book is due out in January 2010 **"Mentoring- Personal Effectiveness "will** assist you in **Personal or Professional Development** and/or give you insight into a new career.

I am also returning to Chester University to complete my MBA – Business Management and gain my Business Advisor Accreditation through Social Enterprise Network. Also I am waiting to hear in news regarding the role as Board Member of Social Enterprise Network Board for Chester.

Karen Gould

Application Forms

Most companies now prefer that you complete these on line – so please do as it could be a disadvantage for you if you don't.

Hard Copies

These should be completed in **Black Fine Ink/Pen** and in **Block Capitals** where requested. It must be readable and legible so take your time and concentrate.

Have a hard copy of your CV to hand and on screen to cross check your dates etc

Read the instructions through *carefully*, paying particular attention to the *job description and person specification* – check the latter against their checklist for essential points, that you can complete all those tasks and provide evidence as an example. This will determine your suitability for the position by assessing your skills and qualifications. Please make these work related to be guaranteed an interview through normally a point system. This system is then carried over to the interview stage to score against a selection criteria as used in HR/Search & Selection/recruitment.

A presentation or a test could also be required to support this. PowerPoint is preferred now – so it is necessary to have these skills or develops your skills.

Psychometric testing could then be used too prior to interview selection or on the day of the interview (see Selby & Mills which is favoured by most Public sector organisations and practice, practice, practice).

For each point assessed you can drawn upon Voluntary experience as an example, remember you are being assessed on your ability to do the job! Always give an example such as;

Good communication skills rather than I have the ability to communicate – this is not sufficient!

As an experienced Trainer I have developed excellent communication skills through delivering training to diverse groups and from my presentations to Corporate Companies re Donor Fundraising. Also, conducting personal appraisals to internal staff.

Read through their advice on completing the form and use their checklist at the end to double check for enclosures before sending;

Example

Equal Opportunities Monitoring Form. Each company has clear policies on the above and now **diversity** plays a big part in this – so please complete accurately and honestly.

Confidentiality/Discrimination Form. This is a workforce audit form and you must indicate any disabilities/medical conditions that could affect your work and to assist you at interview.

Ethnic Origin. Normally consistent with the ONS 2001 census.

Please make sure you put the job title and reference number on each form as sometimes they are separate from the main application form.

Personal Details

- Full name including any middle names, or names you have been known as in professional life.
- Full postal address including your postal code.
- Contact details – include a land line and mobile number and an email address – professional. Make sure they can contact you quickly to set up an interview.

You may have to provide National Insurance number and you Date of Birth – make sure these are correct. More recently there is a question relating to you residency and eligibility to work in this country and you make be asked to provide evidence at the interview stage. You may use a valid British Passport, your NI card or a Driving Licence but please check their requirements.

Education

Always in date order, most recent first and again you have your CV for this to copy from and check dates etc.

Training

Give relevant training details, most recent first. Use this to demonstrate your personal development and any professional bodies that you belong to.

Present Employer

If you are unemployed, put in voluntary work.

Make sure any salary, pay scale and dates are put in and when you can start – all indicate whether you are suitable for an interview.

Previous Work Experience

Date order with most recent first. Make sure it corresponds with your CV and explain any long gaps of 6 months or more.

Voluntary Work

Include any Community work and working from home etc

Criminal Background

Always give a Yes/No answer, never leave blank and make sure you sign it and date it. If you answer Yes you need to check whether spent/unspent depending on the nature of job. If in doubt contact their HR/Line Manager of the Department to discuss in confidence.

Job Share

Indicate Yes/No – they sometimes have people listed who want job share.

Asylum and Immigration Act 1996

Do you have a work permit? Yes/No

Declaration

A signature is always required. Without signing and dating it – it is not valid.

NOW! Get someone to proof read it and get their comments before sending it off.

I always do one in rough or in pencil and sometimes have to have 3-4 attempts.

GOOD LUCK!

Business Letters to support your Application Forms

You will usually need a covering letter for your CV so we use a standard Business Informal letter style which is blocked and unpunctuated.

Again, use your spell check and ask someone to proof read before you send it off.

In this exercise we aim to:

Eliminate those:

- spelling errors
- grammatical mistakes
- general untidiness

Enhance your presentation:

- demonstrate attention to detail
- highlight those strengths
- showcase the pride you take in your work!

Do;

Make sure the letter supports the job description and highlight some of the words they have used within it and demonstrate your knowledge and experience of this in your letter.

Print off your letter, read it through several times or email it to a friend/mentor for suggestions.

This is your opportunity to say more in a supporting letter than is in your CV and demonstrate your IT and communication skills

Don't:

Display any weaknesses – this states that you do not produce quality work or pay attention to detail.

Finally, it should be on 1 page and be to the point and factual.

The following pages are a sample of a completed Application Form

Staff Application Form

This form is available in alternative formats e.g. Braille, large print, disc and on-line

To enable us to process your application, this form and the Equal Opportunity form must be completed and returned by the closing date to Personnel, Liverpool John Moores University, Rodney House,

70 Mount Pleasant, Liverpool L3 5UX. (Email: - jobs@ljmu.ac.uk). Can you please?
- Complete the form legibly using black ink, biro or typeset
- Write the vacancy reference number and candidate number on all pages as the front sheet may be detached from the form. Please ensure any supporting documents are on A4 sheets and securely attached to this form. **Please note the University requires a completed application form.**

Post Applied For		HEAD OF EMPLOYABILITY & UNDERGRADUATE BUSINESS AND MANAGEMENT PROGRAMMES			
Vacancy Ref	**IRC172**	**Candidate No** (if known)			

Section 1   Personal Details

Title (Mr, Mrs, Ms Dr etc)	MS	Surname/Family Name	GOULD	
First Name(s)	KAREN MELONIE			
Address for correspondence	0 ANY STREET WARRINGTON CHESHIRE			
Postcode	WA2 7EN	Email Address		k.gould@hotmail.co.uk

We may need to contact you by phone. If this is acceptable please give the phone numbers where you can be reached or where messages can be left.

Daytime Contact no	079391 64110	Evening Contact no	

Are you aged 65 or over or does your 65th birthday fall within 6 months of the date of your application?   **Yes ☐ No ☐**

Work Permit	
Do you need a work permit to work in the UK?	Yes ☐ No ☐

(UK and EU/EEA citizens do not require work permits) Original documents will be required in the event of an employment offer being made.

Disability

Applications are welcome from disabled people. Do you have a disability that you wish the panel to take into consideration? Where candidates meet the essential criteria appropriate arrangements can be made for an interview. Please give details of any particular requirements

N/A

Application Form for Staff Appointment

Vacancy Reference		Candidate Number	

Section 2   References

All offers of employment are subject to satisfactory references and medical clearance. Please give details of 2 people to whom references may be made, one of who should be your current or most recent employer. Please tell us clearly whether or not we may contact your referees.

	Referee 1	Referee 2
Name	JULIA STICKLEY	DAVID MOWAT
Designation	NORTHERN LIGHTS PROGRAMME MANAGER	CONSERVATIVE PARTY MP - WARRINGTON SOUTH
Address (including postcode)	UCLAN MEDIA FACTORY PRESTON	WARRINGTON CONSERVATIVE PARTY ASSOCIATION STRETTON ROAD WARRINGTON
Tel No	00 000 0000	00 000 0000
Fax No		
Email	Jstickle@anynetwork	dmowat@anynetwork
May not be contacted before interview (please tick)	☐	☐

Checklist

Please ensure that you have either entered/completed:

1	Vacancy Number on all pages of the application form	☐
2	Candidate Number (if known) on all pages of the application form	☐
3	Relevant sections of the application form with signature and date	☐
4	Equal Opportunity Monitoring Form	☐

| 5 | Clearly indicated whether we contact referees | ☐ |
| 6 | Attached supporting documents (excluding CV)
 Please specify: | ☐ |

NB Please note the University requires a completed application form.

Official Use	References Sought	
	Disability Needs	

Comments: please use box below to give us comments on how this form can be improved

Karen Melonie Gould

Application Form for Staff Appointment

Vacancy Reference   **Candidate Number**

Section 3   Education and Training

	Dates	Title/Subject/Grade/Class of Degree Qualification Reg No (e.g. Teaching, Nursing)
GCSE, A' level or equivalent School/College attended: -BENNETT MEMORIAL DIOCESAN SCHOOL FOR GIRLS WEST KENT COLLEGE	1977-79	**6GCSE's - ENGLISH - ARITHMATIC - GEOGRAPHY - CHRISTAIN FAITH - COMMERCE - BUSINESS STUDIES - ENGLISH LANLGUAGE/ENGLISH LITERATURE**
HNC/D/Foundation/First Degree Awarding Institution: REDHILL HIGHER EDUCATION COLLEGE	1985	**FURTHER EDUCATION TEACHERS CERTIFICATE COURSE - CREDIT**
Higher Degree(s) Awarding Institution: BRIGHTON UNIVESITY CHESTER UNIVERSITY	2000 2008/09	**CIPD LEVEL** **MA BUSINESS MANAGEMENT TO COMPLETE**
Professional Qualifications (if any) Awarding Body: ILM	2009	**TUTOR/MEMBER/TRAINER - DIPLOMA LEVEL 5 - LEADERSHIP - MANAGEMENT - MENTORING -COACHING**
Other training Leading to qualifications CITY & GUILDS - TRAINING CERFICATES	2008-09	**LEVEL 3 TRAINERS CERTIFICATE - SAMVOLUNTEER MANAGEMENT DIPLOMA - COACHING PERSONAL/BUSINESSD**
Membership Details of other training or memberships of professional bodies relevant to your application ILM	2009	

Research Publications

Where appropriate please attach a separate list of your publications and/or research interests with this form. Please clearly indicate the Vacancy Reference and Candidate Number (if known)

Application Form for Staff Appointment

Vacancy Reference   **IRC172**   **Candidate Number**

Section 4   Employment Details

Current or Most Recent Employment			
Employer Name & Address	**Position and Duties**	**Employment Details**	
CONSERVATIVE ASSOCIATION PARTY WARRINGTON	BUSINESS/ JOB SEARCH CONSULTANT - WROTE AND DELIVERED JOB SDEARCH AND BUSINESS PROGRAMME - ACHIEVED 10/13 INTO EMPLOYMENT	From	JAN 09 - PRESENT
		To	PRESENT
		Current/Last Salary	£00 per hour
		Leaving Reason	CAREER ADVANCEMENT
		Notice Period	N/A

Past Employment			
Employer Name & Address	**Position and Duties**	**Employment Details**	
MANCHESTER CITY COUNCIL	COMMISSIONING/ PROJECT MANAGER - MANAGED 20 ORGANISATIONS - BUDGETS OF OVER £4M -BUDGETS - REPORTS AND SET UP COMMISSIONING MODEL FOR MCC	From	NOV 08
		To	APR 09
		Leaving Reason	TEMP POSITON

Past Employment			
Employer Name & Address	**Position and Duties**	**Employment Details**	
UCLAN MEDIA FACTORY PRESTON	BUSINESS CONSULTANT - SUPPORTED 5/6 BUSINESSNES IN 08 INTO SME AND DEVELOPMENT THROUGH MENTORING AND TRAINING AND WRITING BIDS	From	JAN 07
		To	PRESENT
		Leaving Reason	CAREER DEVELOPMENT

Karen Melonie Gould

Employer Name & Address	Position and Duties	Employment Details	
YMCA WARRINGTON	FUNDRAISING/BUSINESS DEVELOPMENT MANAGER - CREATED SUBSTAINABILITY THROUGH BUSINESSDEVELOPMENT AND FUNDING FOR 3YEARS	From	MAR 07
		To	APR 08
		Leaving Reason	CAREER DEVELOPMENT

Employer Name & Address	Position and Duties	Employment Details	
MANCHESTER CITY COUNCIL MANCHESTER	EDUCATION SENIOR COMMUNICATIONS OFFICER - LIASING WITH ALL EDUCATIONAL ESTABLISHMENTS RE CUSTOMER SERVICE	From	APR 07
		To	MAR 08
		Leaving Reason	TEMP POSITION

Application Form for Staff Appointment

Vacancy Reference	IRC172	Candidate Number	

Section 5   Further Information

Further Information

Please use this section to provide evidence of how you meet the person specification and job description criteria. The person specification details the experience, knowledge and abilities, which are necessary to carry out the job.

I have true entrepreneurai blood in my veins , coming from a family history of having their own successful businesses. Indeed these skills and this experience has enabled me to have had 3 companies - a TRAINING & DEVELOPMENT COMPANY - A SOCIAL NETWORKING COMPANY and a Consultancy in SME Business Development and Mentoring. So, I intend to adopt an approach which demonstrates innovation which has created growth for myself and whilst at UCLAN as a Business Mentor created business development for 5/6 of my origianl start-ups.

I can demonstrate a credible change management skill, which is hands on and being that I am a good strategist - work to various methods of strategy from Business Plans - Marketing Plans to having an every day ACTION PLAN - incorporating STAFF DEVELOPMENT through Training and regular communications - whether it is weekly team meetings - email or team building excercises from WORK SHOPS etc.

I set myself goals and set my team-orientated goals and indivudal goals through Appraisals and working to a BUSINESS PLAN/STRATEGY plan ahead and incorporate an element or risk or a continency plan within the BUSINESS PLAN to engage and comfort any problems before they happen - this allows you then to Plan through Budgets. Whilst at MCC - I was responsible for the budgets of 21 projects - £4M and used SAP re Budgets which has 'flag ups' and DASHBOARD to monitor progress and outcomes - these type of tools enable you to plan ahead and keep within budgets.

I have extensive networking contacts, as I personally attend rather a lot of events and meetings in Liverpool - Chester - Manchester - Preston and the North West in general. I attend BUSINESS NETWORK EVENTS - SOCIAL ENTERPRISE EVENTS - E-MARKETING EVENTS - DWP EVENTS and so on - so I have created for myself a database/portoflio of contacts from Educational to Business Links.

I am highly motivated and inspire and motivate others , that is one of the reasons I am able to deliver high outcomes. I have storng leadership skills which I use to influence and persuade to win and secure contracts and form partnerships and new stalkholders. Indeed, whilst working at Liverpool Vision -through events - I have maintained those contacts which I have found supportive over the last few years.

I am a very creative person having created many TRAINING PROGRAMMES from more recently creating a HIGHER EXECUTIVE/GRADUATE TRAINING PROGRAMME in

Warrington - achieved 10/13 into employment and this programme will now be dilvered within Warrington for the next year. Also, your WOW Programme showed a interest in this and I have been in contact with the team there.

I solve problems by facing them before they happen and always have contingency plans to overcome any milstones or barriers. Indeed, whilst delivering the Job Programme - for the next year which will be more gratuate orientated - some of the units have been modified to reflect this - ie - more - e-marketing and soft skills to be added and developed.

I have outstanding interpersonal skills and this will be evident at an interview, but is imperative when working as part of a team as I did at MCC - in a team 20 -where we supported each other.

I have worked in and around employment for the last 20 years and from this experence have a good understanding on how to improve employability. So, on this last course - I introduced a 3 prong attach - BUSINESS MENTORING - PERSONAL EFFECTIVENESS and enabling to coach along and support those unemployed.

Having been recently working at UCLAN with my own HUB - I understand how to work in a modern student centre and the approach required to improve their employablity from increasing awareness of e-marketing - soft skills and recording interactive tasks for students to learn from - it is all about user lead learning which motivates them and puts the responsibility on them to support their own development.

I have a FETC - CREDIT - CIPD - exam not taken due to illness - ILM APPROVED TUTOR/ TRAINER - various training - coaching - mentoring and management certificates and have been accepted to complete my MA BUSINESS ADMINSTRATION at Chester 09 - was accepted last year - but course was cancelled due to numbers. I have also shown an interest in your BA RISK MANAGEMENT COURSE at LJMU as a continegency plan.

I believe strongly that my experience - skills and expertise could take this role to another level and I am looking forward to be contacted for an interview.

PLEASE NOTE: I AM ON HOLIDAY 3/17 August 09.

PLEASE CONTINUE ON A SEPARATE SHEET IF NECESSARY, clearly stating Vacancy Reference and Candidate Number (if known)

Application Form for Staff Appointment

Vacancy Reference		Candidate Number	

Section 6   Further Information

Criminal Convictions

Certain posts are exempt from the rehabilitation of Offenders Act 1974. Applicants for such posts are required to declare all criminal convictions, spent or unspent. This includes any posts where the post holder is likely to have access to children, sick or disabled people (e.g. any posts based on hospital premises) and posts where there is the potential for fraud (e.g. chartered or certified accountants). **This list is not, however, exhaustive and for posts, which fall under the exemption, this will be indicated in the further particulars for the post.** Applicants for such posts must complete the following information.

Have you any criminal convictions (unspent or pending) Yes No

If yes, please give brief details:

Note: the successful applicant for any post exempt from the Rehabilitation of Offenders Act 1974 will be required to give consent for the University to check with the Criminal Records Bureau for the existence and content of any criminal record. Information received from the police will be kept in strict confidence and will be destroyed once the University is satisfied in this regard.

Relationship (if any) with any member of the University staff or Governor	

Canvassing or failure to disclose a relationship to a Governor or employee of LJMU will disqualify your application. Please declare any such relationship.

Please state where you saw the advertisement	

Section 7   Declaration

I confirm that all the information provided, including supplements is correct and understand that any false statement could result in an offer of employment being withdrawn or in termination of employment.

(If sending this form electronically pleases type your name in the signature box below to indicate you have read and agree with this declaration.)

Signature   KAREN GOULD   Date   22 July 09

Data protection Act 1998: Some of the data which is given on this form will be entered onto a computer database for the purpose of recruitment administration and equal opportunity monitoring. All application forms except for the appointed candidate will be shredded after 6 months in compliance with University policy.

Please note that all appointments are subject to receipt of satisfactory references and medical clearance and/or risk assessment. Some posts may be subject to a police check.

Karen Melonie Gould

For Official Use Only

Please ask candidate to provide telephone number where they may be contacted following the interview.

Name of Candidate   Tel No.:

Email Response

This can be used to send your CV or Personal Profile to an advertised position or for speculative research.

Example

Dear

With reference to the above vacancy as advertised in the Liverpool Echo dated 30 Nov 09, I have pleasure in enclosing my CV as requested.

or

I have noticed from reading your success story (Congratulations!) in the Liverpool Echo dated 30 Nov 09, that you have been awarded £10M in funding for future development of Training for R2R Programmes. I am enclosing my CV for your attention for any positions in this area.

Now, continue using adjectives from the JD from the advertisement to give support to your CV and giving evidence.

or

To support your speculative response please give relevant experience of date to support CV.

I am looking forward to hearing from you with regards to an interview.

or

I would welcome the opportunity to discuss further over a coffee any future career opportunities.

Regards
Karen Gould (Ms)
k.gould@hotmail.co.uk
00 000 0000 (m)

The Hidden Job Market – E-Marketing

Based on Chris Cardell's Sunday Times and BBC appearances on Entrepreneurial Success, his Marketing Strategy aims to increase your Business Success from 50% to 250%.

Top Ten Tips

1. Stop wasting time – Do not rely on advertisements, there is the HIDDEN JOB MARKET to follow up.

2. Be strong and persuasive in your:
   - CV
   - Letters
   - Personal statement
   - Interview technique
   - Confirmation/Contract

3. Build trust, be likeable, add interest

4. Direct response. Richard Branson states that **you** represent yourself, **you** are your own brand, look at your Business cards, letterheads, e mail accounts. They should be professional and have a signature at the end for communications. Use the telephone for introducing yourself – this is me and this is what I do!

5. Use Internet Markets such as Google, E-Market (thanks Marissa Hankinson for her information on Third Marketing). This is the biggest breakthrough in the last century - it allows you to reach out to people – allow you to research them.

   Register your CV with CV sites – Monster etc, Recruitment Agencies such Morgan Hunt, Reed Professionals, Social Networking sites, Facebook, Twitter, Auction Rooms. JCP and DWP, to name but a few.

6. Have a traceable, factual work history and references. Deliver and reassure based on trust and honesty.

7. What's in it for me? Being selfish? We think the whole world revolves around us. Think of the quality of the service you give, benefits to the company – LEARN their needs and understand their history.

8. Strategy – be organised, have a work plan

9. Follow up. Don't give up and try again and again. If they have shown an interest, then every month follow this up. 60% of people move on and this creates more vacancies.

10. Don't sell yourself cheap! Only 20% of employers make decisions based on price.

Marketing in today's job market

- Job adverts in newspapers/journals
- Job sites/vacancies on weekly sites – local councils etc
- Job alerts – join alerts from agencies and business links
- Agencies – specialist agencies
- Word of mouth – friends and family
- Job fairs
- Networking events
- Tenders/bids
- Auctions

Hidden job market

- Keeping contacts in your industry
- Canvas companies that demonstrate growth – new contracts – profits
- Attend functions/events
- Email/telephone people/organisations in your industry that have recently been in the national/local press
- Word of mouth, let people know, by a monthly email that you are available and let them recommend you!
- **LinkedIn.com** -This is the way forward, ask your friends and colleagues to join the above and then join the GROUPS Section of your industry.

I have it on the highest authority that due to the ever increasing costs of advertisements and a % fee for Recruitment Agencies, employers use a **search engine** or engage someone in HR or even hire Agencies that specialise in this to source this site to find the suitable candidate and save the employer the time, resources and expense as the potential applicants with a recommendation. www.career4me.com

I was dubious of this but since joining this having elevated my employment opportunities by 40%.

TRY IT – what have you got to lose? And let me know!

Social Media A Glossary of Terms

Third Marketing have pulled together the following glossary of Social Media terms, whether you are a social media guru or you haven't got the slightest idea what a 'tweet 'is, we hope that you find this compilation useful.

Alerts - Alerts can be set up for various terms or phrases to notify an individual whenever those terms appear on the internet in newly published content. Alerts are usually sent to an individual via email.

Blog - Blogs are websites hosting content that is self-published, typically by the owner of the site (blogger). Blogs keep a record of all content updates which are posted to the site in reverse-chronological order (thus the original term, web-logs). Visitors can view the updates on the site or on an aggregator, via RSS feeds.

Bookmarking - Bookmarking means to save a website address for future reference. This can be done individually on an internet browser. An address can also be bookmarked through a social bookmarking site, such as del.icio.us. Social bookmarking allows visitors to comment on and rate the content that is stored there. Other social bookmarking sites include Digg, Stumble Upon and Mixx.

Del.icio.us - Del.icio.ous is a popular social bookmarking site which allows members to share, store and organize their favourite online content.

Digg - Digg is a popular social bookmarking and crowd sourcing site.

Facebook.com - Facebook is a popular social networking site which is free-access. Facebook was initially limited to students with a college email domain but has since expanded to be available to anyone 13 years of age or older.

Flickr - Flickr is a media hosting network where users can upload and share image files.

Forums - Forums are areas on a website which are dedicated to facilitating conversation through comments and message boards.

Friends - Friends, or connections, are individuals who agree to link to one another's profile on a social networking site, such as Facebook or MySpace.

Groups - Groups are micro-communities within a social networking site for individuals who share a particular interest.

Guru.com - Guru is a freelance marketplace. It allows companies to find freelance workers for commissioned work.

Hashtag # - Hashtags are placed in front of words to tag or categorise a post. Hashtags are used on Twitter to group tweets and more easily follow discussion topics.

LinkedIn.com - LinkedIn is a social networking site. Much like Facebook, LinkedIn allows members to connect with other users on the network, although LinkedIn is geared more toward professional connections.

Meetup.com - Meetup.com is an online social networking portal that facilitates offline group meetings in various localities around the world. Meetup allows members to find and join groups unified by a common interest, such as politics, books, games, movies, health, pets, careers or hobbies. Users enter their city outside and the topic they want to meet about, and the website helps them arrange a place and time to meet. Topic listings are also available for users who only enter a location.

Micro-blog - A micro-blog is a social media utility where users can share small status updates and information. Micro-blogs combine aspects of blogs (personalized web posting) and aspects of social networking sites (making and tracking connections, or "friends").

Mixx - Mixx is a user-driven social media web site that serves to help users submit or find content by peers based on interest and location.

MySpace - MySpace is a social networking community. MySpace allows more freedom for users to personalize their profiles than other social networking sites, such as Facebook, which are more structured.

Peer-to-peer - Peer-to-peer refers to any type of interaction between two or more people within a specific social network. Oftentimes the term is associated with file sharing.

Podcast - A podcast is audio or video content which can be downloaded and listened to or viewed offline. Podcasts are often created to provide copies of radio or television programming, as well as to accompany internet press releases.

Profile - A profile is a personal page within a social network created by a user. The profile provides information about the user and often links to the profiles of the user's friends.

Registration - Registration refers to the process of signing up to participate in an online social media network or community.

RSS - RSS stands for Really Simple Syndication (or Rich Site Summary). RSS feeds allow users to subscribe to content updates on their favourite blogs and websites.

Slideshare.net - SlideShare is the world's largest community for sharing presentations. Individuals and organisations upload presentations to share their ideas, connect with others, and generate leads for their businesses. Anyone can find presentations on topics that interest them. They can tag, download, or embed presentations into their own blogs & websites.

Social Media - Social media refers to all online tools that are available for users to generate content and communicate through the internet. This includes blogs, social networks, file hosting site and bookmarking sites.

Social Network - A social network is a site or community on the internet where members can interact with one another and share content.

StumpleUpon - StumbleUpon is an Internet community that allows its users to discover and rate Web pages, photos, and videos.

Subscribing - Subscribing is the process of adding an RSS feed to an aggregator.

Tags - Tags are a list of keywords which are attached to bookmarked content, a blog post or a media file. The tags are used to help categorize the content.

Tweet - A tweet refers to an entry made on the micro-blogging site, Twitter. Tweets can be status updates, informative or even include links and can be up to 140 characters long.

Twitter.com - Twitter is a micro-blogging platform which allows users to create profiles and follow other users as friends, much like a social networking site.

VisualCV.com - VisualCV is a free multimedia online CV that allows you to add images, charts, references, awards and much more.

How to find a job on Twitter

Tough economic times call for innovative approaches. An estimated 51 million people internationally are expected to lose their jobs in 2009, and with the unemployment rate on the rise, how do you find career opportunities fast? One great option is Twitter. Twitter is evolving as another resource, in addition to traditional methods, for both job searching and recruiting. Why not follow the steps below:-

1. **Make your Twitter presence "employer-friendly"**
   - Put your job pitch in your Twitter bio (which is 160 characters)
   - Use a professional looking avatar
   - Tweet about your job search

2. **Utilize your Twitter background**. There's lots of space you can use to promote yourself. Don't know how to create a professional-looking Twitter background? Use this free template to design your own.

3. **Include a link to an online CV** or resume in your bio. Use a tool like VisualCV.

4. **Establish yourself as an expert** in your field on Twitter. It's important to note that you should **not** misrepresent yourself. If you're not a medical doctor, don't play one on Twitter. As those on Twitter become interested in your content, when employers are looking at you, you'll have more than just your resume to back up your knowledge and experience.
   How do you get to know the right people? It's not always about who you're looking for; some people on Twitter are actually looking for YOU. There are many job recruiters who use Twitter to look for potential candidates. Before contacting a recruiter via Twitter, check out:

   - Their bio
   - Follower/Following ratio (Have they been around a while? Do they follow people back?)
   - Click the link to their website
   - Ask others in your network whether or not the recruiter is a credible source

Job search tools & resources

A reactive job search on Twitter probably isn't the best way to find a job. There are many new Twitter tools and applications to assist with a proactive job search.

@Microjobs - Started by well-known PR professional, Brian Solis, @Microjobs was developed to bring together job seekers and recruiters through tweets. Recruiters begin their tweets with @ Microjobs, and then submit. The @Microjobs account automatically tweets out requests to its growing network of job seekers.

TweetMyJobs - Another tool born out of Twitter for job seekers and recruiters. Follow the hashtag #Tweetmyjobs and visit the website. This is a very simple (and free) tool for job seekers. You can subscribe to desired job channels and even have new openings automatically sent to your mobile phone. Even better? You can specify which cities you want notifications from.

Job search accounts

There are a variety of Twitter accounts dedicated to providing job listings by field, company, region, and more. Here are just a few to get you started.

@thirdsectorjobs – Jobs in the Voluntary Sector
@sciencejobs_UK – Jobs within the Sciences
@twitjobs – range of sectors advertising a multitude of roles
@JobMote_Ruby – recruitment agency based in Manchester
@Warringtonjobs – Jobs within the Warrington Area
@jobworld – recruitment agency operating throughout the UK

To find additional Twitter job resources, use the Twitter search function and type in keywords such as "job openings," "looking for a job," or "healthcare career." Your next job could be just a tweet away. *Source: Mashable*

THIRDMARKETING

Finding a job through Social Media

Everyone knows that job candidates are flooding the market right now. There are jobs out there, but standing out in a sea of experienced, qualified applicants can be difficult, but not impossible. Social media offers a plethora of opportunities for marketers to reach consumers and businesses, but it also offers job candidates a direct line of communication to corporations and hiring managers. Here are some tips for would-be new hires - both to stand out in the crowd and find the job opportunities leveraging social media:

1. Clean Up Your Online Image - First and foremost, make sure that your online image is Google-ready. Most hiring managers will Google a job candidate at some point in the hiring process - sometimes before an interview. Google yourself and find out what happens. Is your LinkedIn profile up to date? Has your personal blog been dormant for months? Do photos from a night of over indulging in Cancun come up in search results? Take a good inventory of how you appear online and prepare the groundwork. Make sure that content that a potential employer can access is appropriate. Use privacy settings whenever possible. Untag yourself in photos if you can't remove them from the public eye. Ask people to recommend you on sites that allow reviews such as LinkedIn and Guru. com. Create new 'favorable' content to hit the top of the search results (see next tip).

2. Make Yourself 'Findable' - If you don't have an online presence, you need one. Social media is a great way to quickly create an online reputation for yourself and build out your resume and profile. Most of the tools are free. Create a LinkedIn profile, a Facebook page, join Twitter and any relevant professional networks or communities in your field. Even adding your name to a directory or commenting on a high profile blog can create new content for a prospect employer to find when searching for information on you. You can create a YouTube video of yourself (but make sure it's industry/job appropriate) or a full website resume.

3. Be an Expert - In addition to looking for job opportunities, you should be looking for opportunities to put your skills into action. Consider starting a blog or at least, a guest blog to highlight your field of knowledge. Create an online portfolio of your work with a Flickr account. If you are a marketer, answer questions on LinkedIn pertaining to marketing (this also puts your name and business smarts in front of all of your connections.) Participate in message boards and forums that are frequented by prospective employers and be a helpful presence - answer questions, post articles, start discussions, etc. Focus your 'tweets' on Twitter to build a following in your field. Share your ideas, best practices, relevant articles and other information that 'prove' you are in the know

and have up to date skills to share. Post PowerPoint presentations on SlideShare to show off your handiwork.

4. Join the Group - Groups on LinkedIn, Facebook and other platforms offer more opportunities to connect with potential employers and colleagues. When you join a group on LinkedIn, you are often able to direct message members. This can be a direct line of communication to a hiring manager or executive at the firm of your desire. When appropriate, you can also post message to the entire group to help in your job search. In addition to groups, a single connection may be your gateway to the right job opportunity. Leverage individual connections to facilitate introductions to hiring managers.

5. Actively Listen - Don't just rely on the traditional job boards to find your next position. Set up RSS feeds and Google Alerts to notify you when new jobs have been posted in your field. Check out non-traditional job boards. For example, LinkedIn also has job boards inside group settings where only group members can post job opportunities. If you 'fan' a company on Facebook, you might be the first to find out about job openings. Seek out and follow recruiters (professional recruiters and internal hiring managers) on Twitter. Many often post job opportunities on Twitter first before sending out mass communications to their network. In addition, responding via Twitter may separate you from the 'death by inbox' syndrome that plunges many resumes into the email abyss.

6. Turn Online Connections Into Offline Connections - Social media offers us opportunities to expand our Dunbar Number (theoretical number of sustainable social relationships that one person can maintain) from 150 to hundreds of thousands. However, when it comes to getting a job, candidates are usually only hired after they've met the hiring manager in person. And, influencers still tend to recommend candidates that they know and have met directly. So, take your online relationships offline. Participate in networking events, organize a MeetUp, take a connection out to lunch and ask for informational interviews to get some face-time with potential employers.

Confidence Building

On the way to self confidence is Reinvention

For those of us who have been made redundant or face redundancy, this is a 'true awakening' as we think we know ourselves!

It is surprising how differently we see ourselves compared to how other people see us. Our friends and relatives may see us as strong, intelligent people, but sometimes in our work, we lose ourselves – we get used to acting out a role and neglect who we truly are. We can then become trapped within a role which is not what we are comfortable with.

Making changes

Psychologist Timothy Butler in his book" Getting Unstuck", states that this is a **psychological impasse' being stuck or paralysed.** You may now desperate to change in order to find work and the best way out of '**impasse**' is to **Reinvent yourself!**

Celebrities who have reinvented themselves;

- Madonna
- David Beckham
- Catherine Zeta Jones
- Politicians and entrepreneurs and many more

Exercise - Reinvention;

Write a list of all the people you know who have reinvented themselves.

This is not a PR gimmick– if you do not write your list you cannot move on in your life and you are limiting yourself. If celebrities can do it – **so can you!** – stay relevant to your audience of work!

Finding the real you

This normally starts with your **appearance** – this is your branding! This should be a reflection of inner self and requires action. Clearing out your wardrobe is a start. Visit life coaching at beyondonline. org

Exercise – Branding;

You must have a clear understanding of who you are to do this exercise.

Write a list of the following headings and descriptive words related to how you feel about each one:

Work Family Health Love Friends Creativity Spirituality

NOW take a look at the words- are you proud, frustrated or surprised at any of the words that define you?

Author of your own biography

Dr David Lewis in his book The Mind Lab, defines that reinvention is that **you** are the author of your own biography!

Exercise- Choices;

Write down the three main choices you made in your life – did you make them or did someone, or something, play a major role in this? For example; Going to University? Were you in control at that time? Was it a **positive/negative** impact?

If you had made some different choices would your life be different now?

That is the SELF you left behind.. How do you feel about that SELF?

Are you relieved or do you envy the person you left behind?

NOW – base the above exercise on your future decisions to help you make the right decisions.

Know yourself – the Employee

What have you done in the last 12 months which you are proud of?

Now, imagine one year from now what you could achieve and that you feel you would be proud of?

Is this a **contribution t**o your Life?

Know your audience – the Employer

People that have an effect on the decisions we make are called 'stakeholders' and it does not mean they always work in our favour or interest. You must stay in control and imagine how they see your strengths/weaknesses (areas for development) if they do not have vision they are unable to see you for your strengths but they do see you for their own game.

Karen Melonie Gould

Positive Thinking – Reinvent Yourself

Protect yourself from negative emotional contagion and develop a positive new outlook. We need to be able to lift ourselves out of a NATIONAL GLOOM!

There is a financial crisis, though we must not panic even though are concerns are valid, we don't want to become mob handed or indeed invest in the drama that is surrounding us at present.

Conversation

It is hard at present to avoid having a conversation which does not revolve around the above and, though research suggests that this is neither healthy nor beneficial. If you collectively discuss the above then there is the possibility you will become depressed and anxiety will set in. So, concentrate on the job around you, laugh with friends and family and if you are happy everyone around you becomes happy – is infectious! The rush of the **'feel good'** factor is something to be shared and this **'karma'** then brushes off onto others.

Take out the feelings of cynicism and replace them with feelings of hope, love and optimism! Human beings need inspiration from self or others and this works positively within the dynamics of the group at job club.

Elevation evokes us to lead a more positive life and the above gives us the desire to do so.

Reset Button

Robert Biswas-Diener, Author of "Happiness - Positive Psychology" focuses on things that being unemployed cannot take away from you;

- positive thoughts
- strengths
- loyal
- positive
- happy
- kind
- motivating

These traits will help us thrive in this economic downturn.

Identify with your strengths and stay focused on these and you will leave your depression behind you and will be happier. I cannot stress enough, spend any spare cash on an experience – go listen to a guest speaker, attend at event, social networking, courses etc not another coffee in your favourite coffee shop!

Laughing

Laughing is contagious and as the saying goes 'when we laugh, the whole world laughs with you' when we laugh we remain positive and send out positive signals to pick up 'good will'. When you are low and negative you will send out negative signals because your mind is rigid.

- Open up your mind
- Ease up
- Relax
- Accept yourself

See Dr Michael Sinclair – Director of CITY Psychology Group

Ways to be positive

1. Stop complaining and listening to complaints – only give positive criticism.
2. Read only success stories – people doing well in their career, sport, business etc
3. Join a group – we become more competitive and need the support of others
4. Share resources - by pooling your skills and sharing these this builds networks and enhances your strengths.
5. Volunteer – Support a group within your community, one you are inspired by.
6. Explore – explore – explore!
7. Be adventurous – try new things, this generates positive thoughts. Meeting new people will BOOST YOUR POSITIVE ENERGY!
8. Join a gym – take an opportunity to trial for a week free of charge.
9. Creates new contacts – new topics and new OPPORTUNITIES!

NOW – here is your challenge!

Let us CASCADE our HAPPINESS to our friends and family and BE DARING and start conversations which are POSITIVE!

Exercise

Write a list of how not to start at conversation (negative conversation)

Write a list on how to start a positive conversation

This exercise leads into ASSERTIVENESS by knowing how to stop negative conversations or changing conversations which are leading nowhere.

BE BRAVE AND TRY IT!

Branding

Branding – The Real Me (Saturday 13th February 2010)

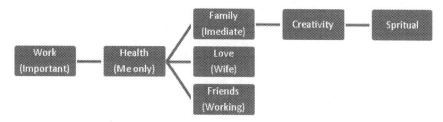

Branding – The Changed Me To be continued !!!!

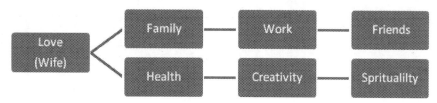

What I consider my:

Strengths
Good Communicator
IT Skills
Creative
Good Engineering Knowledge
Goods Sales Knowledge
Excellent Time Keeping
Organised
Motivated by work
Can work under pressure
Enthusiastic
Innovative
Hard Worker
Team Player
Forward Thinker
Multi Skilled
Flexible
Passion to do a Job Well
Determined
Reliable / Good Time Keeping
Conscientious

Weakness
Impatient - Has to be done now
Do the work rather than delegate – it's quicker
Always think I'm right
Sometime's comes across as negative
Say what I think – don't hold back?
Take on too much/volunteer too much
Sometimes Jump the gun
Sometimes a little shy
Written skills

My 12 Month ACTION PLAN

Make time for my family

- Listen
- Love - Extra Speacial Wife
- Special Daughter/Grandaughter
- Smile more
- help
- Support
- Dont pick up the Blackberry when on holiday

Health

- Be positive
- Make time for excercise, walk at least 4 miles a day
- Encourage others to do the same
- Make time for myself

Creativity

- Find the Right job that is for me and not somthing that will fit the gap
- Work hard but at the same time keeping in mind that family matters
- look at ways to prevent constant stress in the work enviroment
- Manage the day better

Friends

- Forget the past and move on, gather new friends by social networking.
- Remember those that you thought had let you down were only protecting there own jobs and had nothing against me as an individual.
- Move on from those Negative people in your life

Leadership

These notes are based on NHS Leadership Framework Model.

Through Group discussion state what the following mean

- self belief
- self awareness
- self management
- drive for improvement
- personal integrity

An extract from the NWDA – Northwest Regional Economic Strategy 2006;

To develop leadership, management and enterprise skills and develop world class management/leadership and corporate social responsibility/environmental management skills by:

Focussing support on managers of companies looking to grow and 1st line management/supervisory staff with no formal management training.

Developing the Northern Leadership Academy, strengthening the network of Leadership Centres and Development Programmes, and developing mentoring opportunities.

Research

This indicates that management/leadership and work organisation skills are crucial for companies, ensuring the skills/ideas of the whole workforce are used effectively. Key issues include developing the demand for leadership skills and considering making leadership development a condition of taking up business support grants.

Suggested books to read

Edward de Bona and Robert Heller, Management Intelligence – sign up for email alerts

Richard Branson and Warren Buffett, Thinking Manager Style – this is the one I personally would go for!

Richard Branson, British Entrepreneur. The Virgin Group has over 200 companies in entertainment, media and travel with an estimated fortune of £4 billion he certainly made the Rich List 2006.

Having worked and professionally interacted with NHS.NWDA and Richard Branson I will most definitely go for Richard Branson as its hands on.

Get things done now, not later and delegate!

Richard Branson puts his success down to **time management skills** and feels that in the beginning the following skills crucial to leadership qualities:

- upbringing – stand on your own two feet
- character building – endurance
- believe 100% in yourself
- be proud
- strong personality
- build from scratch
- trail & error
- time management skills – 1/3 on trouble shouting,1/3 on new projects (charitable/business) and 1/3 on marketing
- time for family – holiday and friends
- social responsibility
- delegation
- caring personality – people matter, like people it will bring out the best in them.
- step back
- the department/company must be able to operate smoothly without you!

Management Skills

We will focus on two types of MANAGEMENT STYLES and you decide what you are more comfortable with – if any at all!

Predictive management skills

To prevent problems and focus on problems not arising!

You tend to be:

- thoughtful
- analytical
- not looking for dramas/problems
- able to concentrate on what is happening at present
- what is important
- can identify patterns of errors
- more focussed on what went wrong
- has a need to fix it
- always looks at the bigger picture
- works through all the details

If you have the above qualities then you are a DETACHED person who can identify and implement, relate and link to the early warning signs!

Reactive management skills

Solves problems as they occur and gets resources back on track

You tend to be:

- decisive
- can act quickly
- can find solutions
- creative
- creates solutions
- innovative
- calm
- in control
- analytical

You can be both, or start off as a reactive manage and develop into a predictive manager

Exercise- are you a good manager?;

Need to get better at predictive management? So practice!

You had a problem at work:

What happened? Any signs? What did you do? What could you have done to prevent it? What can you do to prevent it happening again?

A good manager continually monitors to flag up warning signs and then evaluates results! Learn from your skills as a reactive manager put your resources into 'getting things done'! in preventive management – give yourself time to think!

Action Plan II

(Listed in order of priority – remember **time management**)

You should start your working week with a 7 am rise with breathing exercises, a 10 minute exercise plan followed by light healthy breakfast. Wash and dress and be ready for a working day. Sample of my day;

1. Clear out emails and respond.
2. Send 5 speculative emails to success stories that I have read about over the weekend.
3. Application 1 – Social Network Board
    Each day you should break for a light lunch and a good walk.

4. Visit to solicitors, dentist, doctors
5. Try to create contacts – email or phone
6. 2nd application
7. Re-evaluate CV, letters and personal profile
8. After 10am visit all **job sites** ie Councils etc and note job vacancies
9. Social Networking Event – Liverpool – Fundraising Event – BT
10. Gym – banking
11. **Job club** – family/home/leisure activity
12. Support family members and prepare **Action Plan** for following week.

Additional Tips

Look up old work colleagues, check local council sites and agencies for successful tenders to demonstrate NEW contracts.

Interview Techniques - Steps 1 to 23

'Get the job you deserve'!

You are advised to have a **strategy** for this and can use various methods:

- **behavioural**
- **NLP**
- **emotional intelligence**

Or, why not combine all of the above:

I am going to take you through this **last but one hurdle in steps**! Personally this is the most nerve racking and unpredictable experiences of the whole procedure of securing a job!

Step 1

You receive your confirmation of your interview in writing by post, letter, email, telephone call or text or in person.

Action

Confirmation

If you ring to confirm please speak to the person direct and follow this up in writing by letter or email **thanking** them for inviting you and **confirm** correct date, day, time and place. **Ask** for directions and best possible means of transport i.e parking etc so you can plan your journey. **Ask** who is on the panel, their names, titles etc to research these people within the organisation or outside the organisation. **Ask** about the format of the **interview, presentation title** – clarify this with them and check for much time has been allocated to this as part of the interview. **Ask** how long will the interview be. **Ask** how many candidates are they interviewing and if there will be 2nd or even 3rd interviews. **Ask** if anyone is being interviewed who is internal or on redeployment? **Ask** do they want to see any additional information i. e. certificates

Step 2

Action

Research company

Go to their website, research the people who are interviewing you and even call them for additional information or just to familiarise yourself with their voice, response to questions and information given. Do you know anyone in the organisation who can give you some internal politics on the Team, Department and Company etc?

Know as much as possible about the people and the company before you go:

- products/services
- new areas of investment

- their vision
- development
- structure

Do you fit in? **Ask** someone who already works there

What is **corporate integrity?** Visit one morning and watch who goes in, the style of clothes, type of person and SPOT any trend or branding going on

You want to fit in!

Step 3

Action
'Think Positively'
This is the physiological approach to the interview-! Think positively about the organisation, the people and your JOB ROLE!

Step 4

Action
Create an Impression
This is all about impression. Remember that the first impression is the lasting impression! Again from doing your research or visiting the company you will see what **corporate dress code** is and what is not.
Clothes
Go to your **corporate wardrobe** and co-ordinate the outfit to suit the image, being comfortable to suit the weather. A good colour choice is black, navy blue or grey teamed with white, red or purple to make an impact. Does your suit need to go to the dry cleaners? Do it now! Should you buy a new shirt/top to make you feel good about yourself, because you are worth it? Shoes – are they in good condition, do they need to be heeded? Accessories – do not over do it, that goes for jewellery, scarves etc. Files – do you have a briefcase or a case trolley? Do not use a plastic shopping bag please?

Step 4

Action
Preparation
Make sure you prepare for the journey, have a dummy run and time it – better to be early than too late!

Step 5

Action
Swot Up
The night before read through the **job description, job specification** and other information you have collected. Concentrate on the job specification because it using a point system as in NHS search & selection. So for each point on the job specification you will be asked a question and your answer will be expected to mirror what you put in your application form. Give them a solid demonstration of evidence for that in relation to your last position. Always thinking what skills/qualities you will be

Karen Melonie Gould

bringing to the organisation. If you are preparing a **presentation** using **power point** check that their facilities are compatible with your IT package to make sure you save it in the right format. If you have not done power point for a while go onto an online course or ask a friend to take you through it – there's nothing worse than at the start of interview coming across as 'tacky' and unprofessional.

Step 6

Action
Relaxation
Have a relaxing bath, go to bed early and think positively. Before going to sleep tell yourself "**this job is mine**'! Take some deep breaths and off you go!

- Wake up extra early, have a power shower – a shot of cold water will get your reactive skills going.
- Have a light breakfast and relax.
- Have a check list of what should be in your briefcase; CV, job description, job specification, your certificates and proof of ID. Details of where you are going and how to get there – name of Organisation, address and contact telephone numbers. Take a pen and pad for notes, a laptop if needed. Take your mobile phone but do not forget to switch it off or put it on to silent mode before the interview.
- Leave in plenty time – remember you have done this journey so you have left yourself plenty of time. If it takes 1 hour to get there – then give yourself 2.

I always send my presentation over prior to the interview, the day before I print off a copy and put a copy on my pen drive and take my laptop – so many times has technology failed.

If it is raining take that bloody umbrella – there's nothing worse than arriving like you have been 'shipwrecked'!

Step 7

Action
On Arrival
Arrive 15 minutes before the interview, introduce yourself and ask for the person concerned. YOU ARE NOW ON A STAGE so be nice to everyone, smile and think about what you saying and doing. You can read company literature while you wait, go to the bathroom and freshen up and take some deep breaths – whatever relaxes you.

Step 8

Action
Body Language
Sit up straight, stand up straight and smile! Though, don't smile and shake everyone's hand including the cleaners etc.

Step 9

Action
First Impression
Give a firm handshake making sure your palms are dry, give a warm smile but keep it relaxed. Sit comfortably, get yourself organised, have a glass of water if offered one and you are ready to SELL YOURSELF!

Step 10

Action
Sell Yourself
You are now on stage/on show and you have 2 minutes to make your lasting impression. GO ON – YOU OWN IT!

Note: Names and positions of your interviewers and always give direct eye contact to the person who asks the questions.

Step 11

Action
Timing
Most interviews run from 20 minutes to 1 hour so watch the pace of the interview which will be set by the interviewers. Be aware of the answers you give and do not repeat or waffle!

Step 12

Action
Influence
You must influence from start to finish and stay in control.

Step 13

Action
Rapport
Engage and create this with the interviewers or even one (can be 1-12 on a panel however 3 is average, usually head of your department, HR and the person who you would report to).

Step 14

Action
Pacing
Do not rush or drag out the interview and let them decide when to finish. Even your voice should be paced throughout the interview.

Step 15

Action

Questions/answers

Here are some common ones that keep coming up.

Q: what attracted you to this job?
Q: what qualities can you bring to this job?
Q: give a brief summary of your career to date?
Q: what do you think we do as an organisation and what is our vision?
Q: how do you ensure that monthly reports are completed on time?
Q: how do you ensure that the team members email to you the information you need for the monthly report deadlines?

Your answers will attract a score (sample):

1 excellent
2 good
3 basic
4 poor
0 not applicable

Step 16

Action

Answers

For all of your answers be prepared to give an example and evidence, to back your response and relate it to your last job is possible.

Step 17

Action

Listen

Always listen and influence all of the interviewers but weigh up who carries the casting vote!

Step 18

Action

Do you fit in?

Even though you are thinking positively throughout the interview form a judgement of your own – do you fit in and do you want to fit in? To do this value their eye contact and body language.

Step 19

Action

Interpret the interviewer's needs

Read the signals - give them what they want to hear and not what you want to say.

Step 20

Action
Influence
There are psychological influences taking part here and it is a technique which comes with practice and it helps to build upon rapport!

Step 21

Action
Any Questions?
You must have POWER QUESTIONS to ask? Be aware of the time though?

Examples;

- Your own **personal development** within the organisation?
- **Career Progression** within the role and within the Team?
- Contract – how long and what kind of opportunities are there within the company?

I never ask more than three.

Step 22

Action
Closure
Let the interviewers bring the interview to a close by stating when and how they will let you know.

Step 23

Action
Thank You
Shake hands firmly and thank them for inviting you! Say it with a smile!

You come out feeling on a high and positive that you have done your best and the outcome should be – YOU HAVE THAT JOB!

One of our Mentors, Sheila, was Head of HR at Marks & Spencer and shared this personal insight! TAKE THIS IN GUYS! The shoe being on the other foot!

What Human Resources Managers look for.............

- Ability to do the job
- Make a contribution to effectiveness of organisation
- Potential development

Well done you have worked hard on your CV/application form and this has now paid off by getting you that important interview. Now you need to take the next step by getting suited and booted, plaster on that big smile and be ready to answer a number of questions so that you achieve that job.

HR have shortlisted all the candidates and the interview is an opportunity to assess each applicant. It is also an opportunity for the candidate to ask for more details about the job, the organisation and to make sure it is the right job for you.

Questions should mainly be focused around what you have written in your CV, so:

Be Honest

If you lie or embellish your CV nine times out of ten you will be found out, as there are tell tale signs such as body language (refer to David's session on body language). If you are successful and land the job your lie or embellishment will soon be found out once you are in the role and you could be dismissed.

Know Your CV

Be ready to answer questions on whatever you have written

The format of interviewing is normally based around open questions that start with:

WHO/WHAT/WHERE/WHEN/HOW

Be confident

Not all interviews are taken or attended by someone from HR.

You may also be asked questions that you do not feel entirely comfortable with. If this happens and it makes you feel nervous or uncomfortable take a deep breath before answering and decide how you want to answer.

Ask them to repeat or repeat the question back to the person, you may have misheard what they said.

Chartered Institute of Personnel and Development Survey

In a survey conducted May/June 2009 a number of HR members where asked what they looked for when filling a role.

Flexibility

Fit with culture and values of the organisation

Thank you - Sheila

Follow up that Interview

Okay, so you have secured your 'DREAM JOB' what next – it is not quite over yet. GET IN AND FIT IN!

Step 1
You receive that telephone call to say that you have been accepted for the position subject to satisfactory references. They state that they will put this in writing and check with you the correct contact details of your references. Remember you have these on a separate attached sheet to your CV. Make sure email address and contact numbers are there including mobile number.

You THANK them and await letter of confirmation.

Step 2
Letter of Confirmation arrives stating Start date, time and venue to report and who to report to.

You SEND THEM A LETTER OF CONFIRMATION.

Step 3
In preparation for job check your :

- Transport, Wardrobe, Parking etc

Step 4
Arrive early for your INDUCTION which may be over a period of 1 to 3 days

Step 5
You're CONTRACT and PROBATION PERIOD is normally 6 months – remember that!

Step 6
LISTEN and LEARN

Step 7
Stay focused, be polite and accommodating and GO THAT EXTRA MILE!

Step 8
Arrive early and stay late – do not clock watch

Step 9
Take work home if needed – but anyway – always go home and FURTHER RESEARCH your work and come back for that next day with new information.

Step 10
Attend all meetings – even those out of hours

Step 11

Attend all other events – show interest.

Step 12

Don't step on other's toes – be part of that team – but slowly show initiative.

Step 13

Always be aware of your JOB SPECIFICATION and nail those points.

Step 14

Know who makes the decisions – who shouts the loudest – who really counts and be aware of internal politics and pecking order.

Step 15

Find your feet – feel your way around slowly but surely – STRATEGY – influence!

Step 16

Analysis skills of team and see where you fit in and where the strengths and weaknesses lie – if a weakness of the team is IT – you upgrade your IT SKILLS and show an interest in this and ask the Company to invest in these skills for the benefit of the company and the team

Step 17

Do not get involved in internal gossip – do not take sides and do not gang up on others.

Step 18

No sickness – no holidays

Step 19

Be Punctual

Step 20

After 6 months, prepare your STRATEGY demonstrating what you have achieved in relation to the job specification and take this to your APPRAISAL – then prepare your next 6 month STRATEGY.

Step 21

FOCUS on your own PERSONAL DEVELOPMENT within the structure of the organisation and where you want to be in 12 months from now and how you will get there.

Unsuccessful at an Interview

If you receive confirmation that you have been unsuccessful by whatever means: letter, Email, text, phone, in person or via third parties

Please do not take it PERSONALLY – this feedback it supposed to be objective criticism and positive and highlights those area you need to work on.

Common points raised

- Did not have enough experience
- Did not have as much experience as other candidates
- Other candidates had more IT system knowledge

Sometimes points act as a polite way of saying they just preferred someone else.

Though, whatever they quote please act on it for next time. So if IT SYSTEMS that keeps coming up time and time again then enrol on a course to rectify this problem.

In this economic climate most state that the calibre of candidates was extremely exceptional and it was very hard to come to a decision so please take this that you were suitable – but remember RAPPORT – as someone who was maybe going to be working with you felt that they could work with someone else with more ease.

So, you were not UNSUCCESSFUL – you cannot win the award for the most likeable person all the time!

Recovery time

If they have congratulated you on a polished interview then you are doing the right thing and it is only a matter of time before you will 'NAIL THAT JOB'.

MOVE ON and get back in that driving seat and get back to your JOB SEARCH STRATEGY. This should be done immediately!

If you are devastated, then you need to get over it and MOVE ON – some personal coaches/mentors would encourage you to challenge this decision – though personally the ONLY thing I would do is to practice my interview techniques!

SPEAK TO THE PERSON who made the decision and express your ongoing interest in the role and ask to be kept on file for the future – in case:

They may not survive their PROBATION PERIOD and other vacancies come up within the organisation that you might be suitable for.

Then bring this to a CLOSURE and move on to BETTER AND BIGGER THINGS!

Karen Melonie Gould

Exercise- question asked at interview

Do you wear 'wellies' and what size do you take?

This question took me totally off guard and I answered half of it; Yes I do possess 'wellies' – why?

This question still baffles me and fills me with humour though I did not ask the interviewer the significance of this? However the 'wellie' question remains a mystery to me and what would be your ANSWER and what would be your interpretation of this QUESTION?

ACTION PLAN –Preparation for an Interview

STEPS	ACTIONS	DO'S	DON'TS	RESULT
1	Confirmation	Reciprocate	Ignore	
2	Research	Web/Employees	Make assumptions	
3	Positive thinking	You want the job	What if	
4	Impress	Immaculate dress/firm handshake/ eye contact	Shabby appearance/limp handshake	
5	Preparation	Knowledge/Experience	Leave to last minute	
6	Revise	Company's objectives	Assume	
7	Relax	Breathing techniques	Panic	
8	Early bird	Arrive 15 minutes early	Be late	
9	Body language	Upright/Proud	Irritating habits	
10	Impact	Impress from start to finish	Inconsistent	
11	Sell yourself	Reinforce positive thinking	Weak answers	
12	Timing	Be aware of time	Waffle on	
13	Influence & persuade	You are the one for the job	Take your eyes off the objective	
14	Establish rapport	Likeability	Create an atmosphere	
15	Pace	Have a flow	Be stuck for answers	
16	Q/A	Clear and concise	Negative/now knowing	
17	Examples/evidence	Past work experience	Ramble	
18	Listen	At all times	Confirm questions	
19	Fitting in	Image/branding observe	Ignore corporate image	
20	Interviewer's needs	Not personal needs	List your personal needs	
21	Power questions	1-3 questions, personal development	No mention of money, time off, holidays or breaks etc	
22	Closure	They end interview	You talk on	
23	Lasting impression	Firm handshake-eye contact	Forget to say thank you	

Top 10 jobs in 2010

1. **HR Personnel**
    Earning from £20KTO £100k –very buoyant market – particularly if have a CIPD and employment law - redundancy and re-training.

2. **Construction Worker**
    Particularly Civil Engineers – lots of work in London – South East re the Olympics – skills shortage and housing shortage.

3. **PR Consultants**
    Specialising in Media and Advertising re COMMUNICATIONS and DIRECT MAIL

4. **Teachers**
    Recession Proof and 32,000 vacancies – affordable housing a benefit and training for other Professionals.

5. **Midwives**
    Shortage – increase by 12.5% - as many are now retiring.

6. **IT consultants**
    Outsourcing – work from home

7. **Nurses**
    Shortage – particularly with our growing older population

8. **Accountants**
    With lots of mergers and acquisitions – good time for FINANCIAL ADVISERS too.

9. **Oil workers**
    ABERDEEN is the place to be – with oil prices set to rise and our appetite increases for the fuel.

10. **Market Researchers**
    Particularly, in RETAIL – the need to watch the customer's spend pattern.

Read more by logging onto www. careerbuilder.com – Paul Mackenzie-Cummins

Karen Melonie Gould

Learn to value your own Performance

You can rate your own Interview Performance using a scoring system 1-10 with 10 being highest – if you score below 8 on any – redo your home work.

Research

Did you demonstrate your knowledge about the company? Research format of interview.

Questions/answers

How well did you respond to the questions? Did you give examples? Could you have done better?

Rapport with the interviewer(s)

Did you engage in polite conversation? Were you at ease – did you make them feel comfortable?

Your questions

Were your questions sensible, knowledgeable and asked with enthusiasm? Did you give eye contact with the person who asked you a question?

Follow up that interview

Did you send that letter/email and reinforce your good points?

RESEARCH	Q/A	RAPPORT	YOUR QUESTIONS	FOLLOW UP	TOTAL

TRANSFERABLE SKILLS

Complete a separate worksheet for each job or activity.

For this exercise take your last 3 JOBS and 3 ACTIVITIES – could be VOLUNTARY – Board Membership or other

1. In the Tasks column list each function of your job or activity.
2. Then in the Skills column list the skill you use or used to complete the corresponding task. Here are some examples of transferable skills. Do not limit yourself to the ones listed.
3. In the Skill Level column rate yourself according to your level of competency (1=highly skilled; 2=moderately skilled; 3=needs improvement).
4. Place a * next to those skills which you enjoy using.
5. After you have completed all worksheets, write a list of those skills which you both enjoy using and in which you are highly skilled [1].
6. Then list those skills you both enjoy using and in which you are moderately skilled [2].
7. You can also keep a separate list of those skills in which you need improvement [3] but enjoy using. Set that list aside. These skills need to be added to your Personal Career Development Plan for immediate action.

My Skills		
Job or Activity		
Tasks	Skills	Skill Level

- Plan and arrange events and activities
- Delegate responsibility
- Motivate others
- Attend to visual detail
- Assess and evaluate my own work
- Assess and evaluate others' work
- Deal with obstacles and crises
- Multi-task
- Present written material
- Present material orally
- Manage time
- Repair equipment or machinery

- Keep records
- Handle complaints
- Coordinate fundraising activities
- Coach/Mentoring
- Research Build or construct
- Design buildings, furniture, etc.
- Manage finances
- Speak a foreign language (specify language)
- Use sign language
- Utilize computer software (specify programs)
- Train or teach others
- Identify and manage ethical issues

SO now produce from the exercise above:

1. skills that you like doing and are good at
2. skills that you are moderately good at and are okay with
3. skills that you need to improve and are not so keen on

TABLE ONE

Will give you areas of work you could NOW move into.

TABLE TWO

Will give you areas of work you could with a little polish move into

TABLE THREE

Will give you areas of work you could only move into be taking ACTION in your PCDP.

Now, go back to your STRENGTHS/WEAKNESSES in WEEK ONE – over the past 10 weeks how has this changed – you should have more STRENGHTS in TABLE ONE and LESS WEAKNESSES in TABLE THREE – I hope so!

Employment Strategy until 2010

DATE	OBJECTIVES - AIM	ACTION - HOW	PRIORITIES – 1-4	MILESTONES	OUTCOMES
Nov 7 09	CV X 2 – Personal Profile	Advice mentors and job club	1	IT Access	Polished CV etc
Nov 7 09	Had coffee with Mentor				
Nov 7-09	Voluntary Placement				
Nov 7 09	ACTION PLAN/ STRATEGY				
Nov 14 09	Practice with partner Interview Techniques				
Nov 14 09	Increase Spec Emails x10				
Nov 21 09	Assess DVD – Interview Technique and learn				
Nov 21 09	Increase Social Networking x 2 events				
Nov 28 09	Update knowledge of keeping a job				
Nov 28 09	Join another Networking Club and Agency				

Review this and keep adding to it !

Personal Career Development Plan –
Project Manager 2009/2010

You should always make yourself a career plan:

OBJECTIVE/TARGET/ BASED ON JD/SPEC	ACTION/TASKS TO DELIVER	WHO	BY WHEN	SOURCES OF HELP
To effectively coordinate 3 programmes R2R to generate more monies and increase hours on attended on each Programmes to ensure viability	Liaise with Team Managers to support this strategy – regular meetings and communications. Consultation of process.	All NW Team Managers and Staff.	April 2010	Other Consultants – Programme Appraisals.
To increase number of attendees on each programme to meet with profiles in existing budget	Consult with marketing department re adverts etc Revisit locations and re assess their suitability and accessibility Check existing profiles	Marketing team Landlords Operations /Contract manager	Feb 2010	Trainers Previous evaluation forms
Etc etc				

SME Business Start Ups

From my own personal experience – back in the last recession – I turned my life around and had started two businesses; GOLD INTRODUCTIONS – a social networking Agency, featured on TV,RADIO and various magazines and ADVANCED TRAINING – secured many contracts with LONDON LETEC – BGCC – CONNEXIONS – BRIGHTON UNIVERSITY – and many more.

So, in times of economic downturn and you find yourself without a JOB – this could be the excuse you have been looking for:

Last Year – I yet again found myself in a similar situation and started www.connectconsultancy organisiation.com.

And here I am:

I have for the past 2 years been a **Business Consultant** for UCLAN on their **Northern Lights Project** and last year 5/6 businesses went onto **Business Development.** I was also the **Business Mentor** for **Prince's Trust for Cheshire & Merseyside** and have recently been selected to support the **Business Development Programme for NWDA** in the Wirral and **Social Enterprise in Cheshire and Warrington.**

OKAY – You have an IDEA – maybe it is a hobby of yours which you can turn into a profitable business.

Business Plan

See attached – blank

Finance

See www.businesslink.gov.uk –setting up costs etc.

You book an initial meeting with them and they agree with you:
*   action plan
*   objectives

Before next meeting.

They also give you additional advice on Funding, work opportunities, contacts, events etc. I work with a a dear friend and colleague - an ex banker in the traditional old style – DAVE CHEETAM – BUSINESS LINK who I find truly supportive and encourages me to go all the way even today.

Karen Melonie Gould

WARRINGTON & CHESHIRE SOCIAL ENTERPRISE
For events – networking and FREE TRAINING.
NWDA
Loans for small businesses - £3-50K
For the economic and regeneration of the area.
They have links to BUSINESS LINK and NORTH WEST BUSINESS ANGELS who invest in BUSINESSES from £10-500k

Competitors

Who are you competitors – research then and find out who and what they do and can you compete or other another service/product at a more competitive price and better quality.

It's good to talk

Network and talk to people in your Industry to avoid the unnecessary pitfalls and what would be the potential start up problems. Read: MAKING IT by Lou Gimson and Allison Mitchell and go to www.symagagine.com to talk to other entrepreneurs or log onto www.making it.com.

Can you turn a hobby into a business?

Fitness fanatic? – register at www.excerciseregister.org
Making home-made beauty products - Abide by EU regulations – www.dtpa.org.uk
Cookery - Contact your local Council for FOOD AND HYGIENE COURSES
Jewellery design - See your local University for Courses or visit www.bja.org.uk

Business mentor/coach

Whether you need someone to mentor you who has been in business before or you want a mentor who can work with you on;
- personal assertiveness
- the power of negotiation
- no hardball tactics

This is not a hostile role but an interactive role to try to understand the needs of the person or business.

Set boundaries

Decide on your lower and upper limits - then you know what to expect and what to build upon and when to walk away

Define your relationship

Do not make it personal as they could use these details to exploit you. Distance yourself it is not a friend.

Research

Know what the company are paying and what they get for this – though value your service or goods.

Book – 'HOW WOMEN CAN USE THE POWER OF NEGOTIATION TO GET WHAT THEY WANT' – Linda Babock – Sara Lancaster – Maggie Thatcher!

www.connectconsultancy organisation.com

MENTORING ACADEMY – COACHING – MENTORING – LEADERSHIP AND MANAGEMENT SKILLS ILM LEVEL 3 – delivered through my company.

PERSONAL EFFECTIVENESS MENTORING BOOK to follow in 2010.

Business Plan checklist:
What should your business plan try to include?

- **Business Objectives**

Describe your short, medium and long-term objectives, showing what you want to achieve with your business.

- **Management**

Highlight the work experience, education and qualifications of the Key People that will be relevant to your business. E.g. book-keeping experience, industry experience etc. (possibly a CV if you have one)

- **Premises**

Describe your choice of business premises, including size, location and state of repair and full associated costs. Try to explain why you chose the premises, showing any competitive advantage it may offer.

- **Plant and machinery and equipment**

Detail any existing plant, machinery and equipment you own, showing any outstanding finance and present value. Detail any plant, machinery and equipment you propose to purchase in the future including estimated prices.

- **Products and services**

Describe in detail the main products and services offered by your business, going into enough detail so that someone with no knowledge of your type of business will be able to understand what you are doing. What is unique about your particular products and services?

- **Pricing Your Product or Service**

Describe how you arrived at the price for your product or service. Give a sample of the price(s) you will charge or do charge, showing how your prices compare with your competition.

- **Customers and markets**

Show who, where and how many potential customers you have (locally, regionally or nationally if appropriate). Outline any marketing research that you have that demonstrates a demand for your product, including any information on your competitors.

- **Promotion**

Describe in detail what level of sales you anticipate, showing any firm orders in hand. Also explain what assumptions have been made in making your sales forecast, how you intend to market and advertise your products and services, and why you believe your sales forecasts are realistic.

- **Financial information**

Start-up businesses - Financial projections (at least a cash-flow) for your business including notes explaining your projections.

Existing businesses - As above, but please include any Annual Accounts or Management Information you might also possess.

NB. The Enterprise Fund can supply a blank cash-flow and business plan for you to just fill in if you need it. **e-mail us at info@business-finance-solutions.org.uk**

Chase the Dream – NOW Live the Reality!

Work your way through this book which is based on a Programme I deliver at present for the Conservative Association – 'GET BRITAIN WORKING' campaign in the North West (Warrington). It is a 10 week course based on the accreditation by ILM Level 3 Leadership & Management. It is a bespoke training course to enable you to take the responsibility of your own destination and move forward, onwards and upwards in your life – see www.connectconsultancyorganisation.com.

It is only through working in this industry - assisting people who are unemployed- for over 15 years and working through yet another recession, being unemployed myself and presently, assisting family members who are unemployed – I decided to produce this book so that it becomes your bible and guidance until you get nail that dream!

This model works and on my first PILOT of running a course based on this book produced 11 out of 13 into employment and so on producing 75% overall success rate!

There are some key factors that if you follow this book you will:

Have the tools to confidently go out there in the present job market and nail that DREAM JOB!

- Learn new skills – e-marketing – a must in this economic climate.
- Re-gain your confidence – become positive and assertive in this JOB MARKET
- Learn to evaluate your transferable skills – in order to have a career change if needed.
- Learn to value yourself and your skills and experience and showcase these to perspective employers.

Become … I AM – KAREN GOULD – and I am happy with myself and want to 'nail that DREAM JOB and secure an employment partnership which benefits both! I like my new reinvented groups to give a 3 minute Presentation on the new I AM – so try this with a member of your family or a friend for their appraisal of the NEW YOU!

Now, as you have got this far – it tells me you have a 'CAN DO' attitude and you go out there and 'DO IT' – that you create your own chances and opportunities – I myself needed that inferable 'kick up the arse' and now have my own business once again – a publishing contract – with MENTORING – PERSONAL EFFECTIVENESS out in 2010 – so. I needed to change my life – after have a string of failures behind me and I had to take control and build upon my own self-belief!

If you want this – TAKE ACTION – and it will become a reality! Believe me – if I can do – so can you!

The fact that you got this far – tells me – you are rearing to go!

I have already given you in Chapter 6 , tools for a Weekly/Daily Action Plan and a 1to 12 week EMPLOYMENT STRATEGY – so here we go!

Goal Setting – Achieving your Aims and Objectives

You have the TOOLS - I want you to aim high and just be prepared to go all the way to the top!

You will know whether:

- You will continue on the same career path
- Have a career change – through acknowledging your transferable skills
- Start your own business

If you follow this guide, working your way through this book you will sooner, rather than later receive that JOB OFFER!

Don't delay – do it now – and you will feel much more fulfilled.

Even if you get offered a job which is not your 'dream job' have the confidence to turn it down and move on quickly as I did. Just review what you really want. Why should any of us be 'second best' – be brave – smile and in time just keep believing in yourself as Warren Buffet stated – INDIVIDUALITY – is what he believed in and never let go of this and your time will come.

Then, let me tell you – when your time does come – the elation and sheer pride that you feel - that you can finally share with others and then 'go shout it off the mountain' if you need to - is the word of success – which you can share with others. You have now joined the ELITE CLUB OF SUCCESSFUL PEOPLE – network – break out the champagne and celebrate with joy that you have YOUR DREAM JOB!

This new attitude will shine out and people will stop and ask you – 'what is different with you – you are glowing – please share your secret?

Buy this book now – 'GET BRITAIN WORKING' or log onto www.connectconsultancyorganisation and pre-order the follow up book 'MENTORING – SELF ASSERTIVENESS'.

It happened to me and many of my JOB CLUB members and it will happen to you – it is possible and I and my members have made our dreams our reality!

GOOD LUCK and please get in touch and let me know all your successes!

I wish to share with you for 2009-2010 – our WARRINGTON JOB CLUB members achieved 40/51 -78% EMPLOYMENT OPPORTUNTIES – 10 Business Start Ups – all achieved by following this book/programme. WELL DONE everyone and THANK you to everyone who supported me and will continue to do so.